Designing and Implementing Test Automation Frameworks with QTP

Learn how to design and implement a test automation framework block by block

Ashish Bhargava

BIRMINGHAM - MUMBAI

Designing and Implementing Test Automation Frameworks with QTP

First published: November 2013

Production Reference: 1131113

Published by Packt Publishing Ltd.

Livery Place
35 Livery Street
Birmingham B3 2PB, UK.

ISBN 978-1-78217-102-7

www.packtpub.com

Cover Image by Jarosław Blaminsky (milak6@wp.pl)

Credits

Author
Ashish Bhargava

Reviewers
Selvaraj Gurusamy

Wang Longdong

Dinesh Vijayakumar

Acquisition Editor
Kevin Colaco

Commissioning Editor
Deepika Singh

Technical Editors
Pratik More

Ritika Singh

Copy Editors
Tanvi Gaitonde

Mradula Hegde

Dipti Kapadia

Sayanee Mukherjee

Adithi Shetty

Project Coordinator
Akash Poojary

Proofreader
Chrystal Ding

Indexer
Rekha Nair

Graphics
Abhinash Sahu

Production Coordinator
Adonia Jones

Cover Work
Adonia Jones

About the Author

Ashish Bhargava has over 10 years' experience in Information Technology. Working as a test lead, tester, and Java developer, he delivered many successful applications. He has experience in designing frameworks using various tools and languages. He has worked with HCL Technologies and Microsoft. He worked on QTP, Coded UI, and RFT, and has experience in VBScript, JavaScript, Java, and C#. He has experience in technically mentoring the junior team members to learn automation and test automation tools. He has experience in teaching automation and designing courses for test automation and manual testing. The author is the key contributor at `http://testautomationlabs.com/`.

Ashish has the following professional certifications:

- HP Certified QTP Professional
- ISTQB Certified
- Certified Software Test Manager (CSTM)

Acknowledgments

Though the book bears my name, it truly reflects the collective wisdom of the numerous customers of Mercury Interactive (now taken over by HP) with whom I interacted as a CSO support engineer to resolve their queries related to WinRunner and QTP, and my colleagues with whom I worked. I have learned a lot from them. My many thanks to all of them!

Many thanks to Dinesh and Selvaraj for providing me with valuable inputs to make this book better.

Authors need a lot of support from their publishers. I thank Akash and Deepika for their patience and tolerance towards the mistakes I committed while writing the contents of the book. Salute to Kevin for having faith in my idea of this book.

Lastly, thanks to my parents, and my wife Neeti, who cheered me in good times and encouraged me in bad times.

About the Reviewers

Selvaraj Gurusamy has completed his Bachelor's in Electrical and Electronics Engineering from Sri Ramakrishna Engineering College, Coimbatore, Tamil Nadu. He started his career as a software engineer in the area of Quality Assurance and Testing. Having overall IT industry experience of 8 years, he is presently working as a Test Automation Engineer in Hewlett-Packard GlobalSoft Limited, Bangalore. He has in-depth knowledge on industry-leading automation tools such as QTP and SilkTest. As an automation engineer, he is working on design and development of automation framework, Proof of Concepts, preparing an automation plan and estimation, setting up an automation test environment, and providing guidance and mentoring automation teams. He has received very good feedback and awards from the client/business during his project term, which helped his organization to obtain more automation proposals.

> I would like to thank Ashish Bhargava and Dinesh Vijayakumar for giving me the opportunity to review this book.

Wang Longdong graduated from Xi'an Jiaotong University in 2011, and then learned how to be a test engineer in 51testing. After the lectures in 51testing, he became a junior test engineer. After working hard, he is now an intermediate engineer.

He once conducted lectures about QTP for his colleagues to help them learn automation testing. His interest is now on the Page Objects pattern, which is originated by the Watir-WebDriver. He always has some of his own options about how to design and implement automation testing and likes to be the problem solver for others. Recently he became a freshman on GitHub as a coder for Test Automation with QTP and Selenium.

Dinesh Vijayakumar has done his engineering in Electronics & Communication and has a career in software testing that spans a little over 11 years. He has worked as a tester, module lead, and a test lead, and is currently working as a test consultant with a leading global software company in Hyderabad, India. He has performed various testing activities such as test planning, estimating test efforts, test design, test execution and reporting, test artifact reviews, test automation, and test and project team management in various complex global projects and delivered near defect-free high quality applications to various global customers. He has rich experience in test automation tools such as SilkTest, QTP, and Visual Studio Coded UI Test. He is also experienced in Performance test tool, Loadrunner, and Test Management tools such as Quality Center and TFS. He holds a few testing certifications such as the ISTQB/ISEB certified tester (Foundation), CSTM (Certified Software Test Manager), HP Certified QTP and QC Professional. He is also a PMP (Project Management Professional) from Project Management Institute(PMI).

www.PacktPub.com

Support files, eBooks, discount offers and more

You might want to visit www.PacktPub.com for support files and downloads related to your book.

Did you know that Packt offers eBook versions of every book published, with PDF and ePub files available? You can upgrade to the eBook version at www.PacktPub.com and as a print book customer, you are entitled to a discount on the eBook copy. Get in touch with us at service@packtpub.com for more details.

At www.PacktPub.com, you can also read a collection of free technical articles, sign up for a range of free newsletters and receive exclusive discounts and offers on Packt books and eBooks.

http://PacktLib.PacktPub.com

Do you need instant solutions to your IT questions? PacktLib is Packt's online digital book library. Here, you can access, read and search across Packt's entire library of books.

Why Subscribe?

- Fully searchable across every book published by Packt
- Copy and paste, print and bookmark content
- On demand and accessible via web browser

Free Access for Packt account holders

If you have an account with Packt at www.PacktPub.com, you can use this to access PacktLib today and view nine entirely free books. Simply use your login credentials for immediate access.

Instant Updates on New Packt Books

Get notified! Find out when new books are published by following @PacktEnterprise on Twitter, or the *Packt Enterprise* Facebook page.

Table of Contents

Preface

HP QuickTest Professional is a test automation tool for functional and regression testing for software applications and environments. HP QuickTest Professional supports keyword and scripting interfaces and features a graphical user interface. It uses the Visual Basic Scripting Edition (VBScript) to specify a test procedure and to manipulate the objects and controls of the application under testing.

This book is a great platform for sharing my knowledge of designing and implementing the test automation framework that I have acquired over the years, while working in Information Technology and teaching QTP to professionals. If any professional or student finds it difficult to implement frameworks, this is the right book—one which teaches approaches and concepts with simple examples. This book covers the managerial, technical, and design concepts, and is uniquely designed to deliver the knowledge needed to create an effective framework. It demonstrates easy ways to implement and learn concepts, along with code and suggestions for creating a portable framework across various versions of QTP.

This book also covers the new features for creating test automation using XPath in QTP and JavaScript for automated web applications.

What this book covers

Chapter 1, Automation Life Cycle and Automation Goals, explains the automation life cycle and tool selection which helps to implement better processes for test automation and tool selection. This chapter also explains the overall automation and design goals that help develop a better test automation framework and guides you towards implementing better practices to achieve maximum output.

Chapter 2, Essentials of Automation, explains the key elements for designing test automation using QTP along with examples on how to use each of them. These elements serve as the base to create a complete test automation script.

Chapter 3, Basic Building Blocks for Creating Frameworks, explains the basic code-building blocks (with examples) for designing the implementation of test automation frameworks, all of which are used in implementing the framework(s).

Chapter 4, Understanding and Creating Frameworks, explains what we mean by test automation frameworks and what types of frameworks exist. It guides you towards understanding these frameworks before we design and implement them. The chapter will also highlight the differences and commonalities among them.

It explains the basics of test automation frameworks and builds the user's maturity in implementing test automation framework(s) end-to-end.

Chapter 5, Deploying and Maintaining Frameworks, explains, in the beginning of the design phase, how and what needs to be done to maintain and enhance these frameworks with ease.

Chapter 6, DOM- and XPath-based Framework in Web Applications, explains the various web-based technologies and builds the maturity to implement these technologies for automated web-based applications. It explains HTML, XPath, DOM, JavaScript, and how to use them effectively for creating test automation scripts.

Chapter 7, Capturing the Lessons Learned, explains what should be captured for lessons to be learned and how to make sure that these lessons help in future projects or serve as input in other projects.

What you need for this book

We require the following software to get started with the book:

- QTP 11.0
- Windows XP or Windows 7 32 bit with IE 8
- Patch QTPWEB_00078 for IE 9
- Patch QTP_00699 for Windows 7 64-bit
- Patch QTPWEB_00086 Support for 64-bit IE

 Before installing this patch, install the QTP_00699 patch.

Who this book is for

This book is useful for manual testers, test leads, test architects, automation engineers, and aspiring test automation engineers who want to learn, create, and maintain the framework. It allows them to accelerate the development and adaptation of the test automation framework. This book will equip the tester with the technical and conceptual know-how for creating a framework using QTP.

This book is also useful for those moving from manual testing to test automation and QTP.

Conventions

Code words in text, folder names, filenames, file extensions, pathnames, dummy URLs, and user input are shown as follows: "The `<html>` tag is the root node and it has no parent node."

A block of code is set as follows:

```
Window("WinFlight").WinButton("Insert Order").Click
'Window("WinFlight").WinButton("Button").Click
'When QTP tries to execute the below statement, application will not
allows to click on the button, since it is waiting to reach progress
bar to 100% and display the message Insert Done..
' Here script will fail
' We need  to insert the dynamic synchronization  point and this waits
until the text does not changes to Insert Done…
'Window("WinFlight").ActiveX("ThreedPanelControl").WaitProperty
"text", "Insert Done...", 10000
```

New terms and **important words** are shown in bold. Words that you see on the screen, in menus or dialog boxes for example, appear in the text like this: "Clicking on the **Next** button moves you to the next screen."

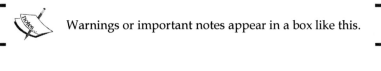

Warnings or important notes appear in a box like this.

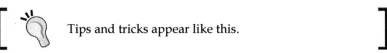

Tips and tricks appear like this.

Reader feedback

Feedback from our readers is always welcome. Let us know what you think about this book—what you liked or may have disliked. Reader feedback is important for us to develop titles that you really get the most out of.

To send us general feedback, simply send an e-mail to feedback@packtpub.com, and mention the book title through the subject of your message.

If there is a topic that you have expertise in and you are interested in either writing or contributing to a book, see our author guide on www.packtpub.com/authors.

Customer support

Now that you are the proud owner of a Packt book, we have a number of things to help you to get the most from your purchase.

Downloading the example code

You can download the example code files for all Packt books you have purchased from your account at http://www.packtpub.com. If you purchased this book elsewhere, you can visit http://www.packtpub.com/support and register to have the files e-mailed directly to you.

Errata

Although we have taken every care to ensure the accuracy of our content, mistakes do happen. If you find a mistake in one of our books—maybe a mistake in the text or the code—we would be grateful if you would report this to us. By doing so, you can save other readers from frustration and help us improve subsequent versions of this book. If you find any errata, please report them by visiting http://www.packtpub.com/support, selecting your book, clicking on the **errata submission form** link, and entering the details of your errata. Once your errata are verified, your submission will be accepted and the errata will be uploaded to our website, or added to any list of existing errata, under the Errata section of that title.

Piracy

Piracy of copyright material on the Internet is an ongoing problem across all media. At Packt, we take the protection of our copyright and licenses very seriously. If you come across any illegal copies of our works, in any form, on the Internet, please provide us with the location address or website name immediately so that we can pursue a remedy.

Please contact us at `copyright@packtpub.com` with a link to the suspected pirated material.

We appreciate your help in protecting our authors, and our ability to bring you valuable content.

Questions

You can contact us at `questions@packtpub.com` if you are having a problem with any aspect of the book, and we will do our best to address it.

1
Automation Life Cycle and Automation Goals

The test automation tool creates a set of scripts that emulates the user action to be performed on the **Application Under Test (AUT)** and replays them over and over with minimal or no human intervention. **Test automation** is a complete process, which goes through distinct phases to automate test cases for applications under the test. The AUT can belong to any technology or domain.

Test automation should start very early in the life cycle of the project and its success depends upon the following:

- Knowledge of the automation life cycle
- Processes in test automation
- Selection of the right tool
- Test automation planning
- Appropriate technical know-how about automation and test automation tools

The key driving and guiding forces for successful test automation are the automation goals, best practices, selection criteria, and attributes for tool selection and processes.

Good knowledge in these areas helps implement the test automation in an effective way.

The test automation life cycle

Test automation life cycle is the process in which test automation progresses through a series of different stages. The focus of this chapter is to learn the key activities and tasks that are performed during each phase of the life cycle.

Feasibility study

A feasibility study is an evaluation and analysis of the potential tool, which can provide the desired solution for the test automation needs of the project(s). The aim is to uncover the strengths and weaknesses of the tool(s) objectively and rationally. Generally, it precedes test automation implementation.

The feasibility study between the manual and automation effort required should be applied based on the following:

- ROI (Return On Investment)
- Future enhancements

Consider the test cases, automation tools, automation environment, development and maintenance of automated tests, skill sets, organizational capabilities, design, and approach of the automation for test automation planning.

The simplest way to define the ROI is *ROI = Benefits/Cost*.

The go/no go decision can be taken after the calculation of the ROI. The future changes in the application/service might possess many threats as well as opportunities for test automation. Leads and managers need to have a clear vision to evaluate the ROI for future enhancements.

The test manager or lead should focus on maximizing the ROI for test automation. He/she should focus on reducing the maintenance cost and achieving faster scalability of the test suite. Computation of the ROI is an important activity, which allows us to foresee many tradeoffs and governs the implementation of test automation. Since computing the ROI is out of scope for this book, this is how far we can go.

Tool induction for automated testing

This phase is designed for successful induction of tool(s) and building the basic infrastructure needed or identifying the needs for test induction.

The key steps in test induction are listed as follows:

1. Identifying the technical/non-technical requirements:
    - The technical requirements are, for example, support for technology, tools, and scripting languages
    - Non-technical requirements are, for example, the goals for test automation

2. Evaluating the tools based on selected attributes along with their respective weightage. Tool evaluation is one of the most technically-challenging tasks when performed with limited knowledge about the tool(s).

   ° Attributes such as user friendliness, license cost, and training cost define tool features

   ° Assign higher weightage (a high number) to the most relevant attributes during tool selection

   Compute the overall score by calculating the sum of the product of weight and value, that is, *Total score* = $\sum$ *Attribute weight* * *Attribute value*. The range of the value may vary, for example from zero to five.

   ° The final selection is based on the final score calculated for the tool(s)

3. Pilot run is when we create the sample scripts to verify that the selected tool is working as expected on the selected test cases. If the pilot run is successful, you can purchase the license or acquire the tool.

Defining a test automation strategy

Test automation strategy is a plan of action designed to achieve the overall aim for test automation. It provides broad guidelines so that the stakeholder knows the approach for design and implementation of the test automation. Few organizations combine the test strategy and test plan in a single document.

Test strategy defines the following:

- Scope
- Framework and design approach
- Script creation approach
- The amount of testing required
- Risk and mitigation plan
- Deliverables

Creating a automation test plan

Planning is the process of thinking and looking ahead for activities and tasks required for test automation. The test plan defines the following:

- Testing architecture
- Tool installation plan

- Test schedule
- Roles and responsibilities
- Resource requirements (hardware, software, and skilled resources)
- Training requirements
- Reviewing the plans for scripts and design documents
- Limitations and assumptions

The test plan document tells us what is to be done for test automation, and when. This document is used by all the stakeholders and it serves as the contractual agreement among the key stakeholders.

Script design and development

This is the key phase where actual things get implemented. This phase requires technical skills for designing the framework and coordination skills to interact with the SMEs (Subject Matter Experts), BAs(Business Analysts), manual testers, and developers to accomplish the various tasks for test automation. The leads have to ensure that the reviews have been done and coding standards followed; the test repository structure is then created and all the resources are kept at appropriate locations. We will create the documents for understanding, using, and enhancing the test automation later.

The key steps in the design and development phase are as follows:

- Analysis and script planning
- Script creation (scripts can be created by recording or manually)
- Creation of common and framework-specific libraries
- Script enhancement (adding exception handlers, checkpoints, and so on)
- Association or integration of libraries and functions with scripts
- Reviews (ensure consistency, coding standards, and version controls are followed as already defined in the plan or strategy document)
- Dry run and analyzing the results
- Debugging the scripts and fixing the defects

Deployment, release, and maintenance

In the previous phase we have performed the dry run; now it is time to deploy the scripts to the appropriate location with a well-defined structure and data. The actual execution may not be carried out by the people who developed the test scripts, as it may be executed by business users, SMEs, or other automation engineers; hence, before releasing the test scripts it should be ensured that all the required documents and automation resources are in place and reviewed by the lead or team members.

The key steps in the deployment, release, and maintenance phase are as follows:

- **Deployment**: After the test automation scripts are deployed, they can be used by automation engineers, SMEs, or even business users
- **Release**: The following artifacts are delivered in this phase (the list may vary based on the project's need)
    ◦ Framework components / scripts
    ◦ Libraries, functions, and data pools
    ◦ Release notes
    ◦ Mapping document (traceability matrix)
    ◦ Design/architecture document
- **Maintenance**: In this phase, we will perform the following:
    ◦ Here we analyze the failures due to scripts or application issues, logs, and fix them
    ◦ We enhance the scripts as per the requirement for each cycle/release
    ◦ The scripts for each cycle are executed

Over a period of time, objects in the GUI and the flow in AUT changes; thus, it is required to change test objects in the **Object Repository** (**OR**) and scripts.

Tool selection

We now need to identify the key requirements, which should cover the depth and breadth of the technology required both at the organizational and project level.

Capturing automation requirements

The requirements for the test automation are gathered from the following:

- Organizational level requirements for test automation
- What technology is used in the organization

- How tools support the automation of these technologies
- Project level or project-specific requirements
- Key technical areas

Developing a POC

The key steps to conducting a **Proof Of Concept** (**POC**) are as follows:

- Identify the minimal test set for POC
- Verify the technical feasibility
- Verify the implementation feasibility if we implement the tools with ease
- Find out if there is any known limitation
- Submit the POC Summary Report

Evaluating the tools

The key steps to evaluating the tools are as follows:

- Identify the key attributes that are most suitable for your project: for example, technology support, technology version, and so on
- Give appropriate weight and value to the attributes; the total score is the sum of the product of weight and value as shown:

  Total score = $\sum$ *Attribute weight * Attribute value*

- The final selection of the tool is based on the total score

Tool selection criteria

The following is a comprehensive-but-not-complete list of attributes that we should look into while considering tool selection:

- **Reliability**: This is the ability of a tool to perform and maintain its functions in routine circumstances, as well as hostile or unexpected circumstances.
- **Capacity**: This refers to the possible output of a system, that is, to create and execute scripts in an efficient and effective way.
- **Learnability**: This tool is quick and easy to learn.
- **Operability**: This is the ability to work under various configurations and environments.

- **Performance**: The accomplishment of a given task is measured against the presently-known standards of accuracy, completeness, throughput, and speed.

- **Compatibility**: This checks whether the tools support various versions of the technology, browsers, or operating systems.

- **Non-intrusiveness**: The key non-intrusiveness features we should look into for tool selection are as follows:

    ° Platform-/OS-independent

    ° Data-driven capability

    ° Customizable reporting

    ° E-mail notifications

    ° Easy debugging and logging

    ° Support for version control

    ° Extensible and customizable (open APIs should be able to integrate with other tools)

    ° Common driver for logging

    ° Support-distributed execution environment

    ° Distributed application support

    ° License and support (cost)

From a broader perspective, test automation is driven by the following:

- The processes defined within an organization
- Design and architecture
- Automation goals
- Best practices for test automation

All of these complement each other for the success of test automation.

Processes

A process can be described as a structured approach to perform various tasks and activities that take place during the automation life cycle. Well-defined processes that are laid out by competent organizations provide the guidance to approach automation, from conception to culmination.

In the absence of well-laid processes and historical data it is difficult to estimate, plan, and implement the test automation. In case an organization is implementing test automation for the first time, it becomes the learning curve for future test automations and provides historical data for future projects.

Design, architecture, and documentation

Well-defined architecture/design helps reduce the overheads and conflicts; it also helps the team to collaborate better and achieve better implementation. The key aspect for designing the solution is to provide abstraction from complexities, encapsulation, and technical challenges. We need to develop support libraries for reusability and expandability of the automation solution.

We have to document the design and architecture. The comments in scripts, script headers, and function headers improve the readability and understandability. Documentation helps in enhancing and maintaining the scripts quickly and easily.

Automation goals

A goal is the desired result that a person envisions. It is the plan and commitment to achieve the desired end point in some sort of assumed development. A goal is the key driving and guiding force for the success of test automation. The design requires breaking the framework solution into components and layers. The automation goals should be met at each level or layer for the overall success of test automation.

The objective of defining goals is to get clarity on the outcome. The goals are defined at each layer and have some cascading effect on each other. They also drive and contribute to each other's success.

Goals for test automation

The overall automation design goals are derived by organizational goals, domains, businesses, and so on. The list may vary from organization to organization. A few of them are as follows:

- Increase reusability
- Enhance test coverage
- Speed up testing for multiple and frequent releases
- Ensure consistency

- Improve the reliability of testing
- Scalability

Goals for framework design

The following is the list of goals for framework design based on the organization, domain, and so on. This list may vary.

- Maintainability
- Readability
- Extensibility
- Reusability
- Application independent
- Should have short driver script/master script

Goals for design

The following is a list of goal design components of the test automation solution or framework based on the organization, domain, and so on:

- The design should be easy to expand and maintain
- It should provide abstraction from complexities
- Identification of the common functions used across scripts
- Decouple complex business functions with utility functions
- Decouple test data and test scripts
- Creation of robust functions
- Appropriate functional decomposition with portability
- Ensure that the scripts are executed without human intervention, even in erroneous conditions
- Design documentation

Goals for script design

The following list of goals for the scripts/code of the test automation is based on the organization, domain, and so on. This list may vary.

- The test should always have a common start point and end point
- It should clean up the resources to be reused, for example, deleting old log files, result files, and so on

- The test should reveal maximum information in case an error occurs
- Configure the values rather than hardcoding
- Appropriate comments and script headers should be present
- The code should be readable and appropriate documentation should be present
- The script should be maintainable and easy to modify
- Error handling and snapshot for errors should be present
- Logging utilities should be available

Setting quantifiable goals

It is essential to set clear, measurable goals for the test automation project. These goals should clearly be brought out. A few examples are:

- The number or percentage of test cases to be automated
- Enhancing the test coverage by percentage or numbers
- Reducing the time to release the build by percentage or numbers
- Reduction of the test cycle time of new releases

It is difficult to get the desired outcome or even the ROI without setting measurable goals; this will lead to a high maintenance cost and the changes to the scripts will cause side effects.

Best practices

Test automation is an integral part of any software development and sustenance project. Some of the best practices that follow will make the test automation project successful.

Choosing the most suitable tool for automation

A misfit tool for test automation increases the effort in designing, creating scripts, and maintaining them, thus increasing the cost of test automation or even failing to achieve the automation goals. Selecting the right tool is winning half the battle. An appropriate tool helps in speeding up script creation, modification, identifying the issues in scripts, and resolving them quickly; in a nutshell, it makes life much easier for the test automation team.

Treating test automation as a development activity

Treat test automation with the same discipline and objectivity as a development project. A successful testing automation project takes a framework-driven approach. Decompose the scripts based on the AUT functionality and divide them into reusable functions. Create a well-defined structure that allows uniform sharing of resources. Prepare appropriate documentation: one that enhances the readability and maintainability. Ensure that the scripting/coding standards have been followed. Finally, you need to test and debug the scripts or code and make sure that the scripts are free from bugs. It is also good to check whether the scripts and resources use version control tools or mechanisms.

Getting the right architecture

It is difficult to extend and maintain the test automation if the framework-driven approach is not used. The overall design becomes chaotic or cumbersome to modify or enhance. The test automation framework allows us to define the scripting methodology to automate tests, create support libraries and common resources to execute the tests, and report the results. Framework allows adding the test cases with minimal effort. It also allows the establishing of a common standard and consistent way to achieve goals for the automation team.

Ensuring relevant and up-to-date test data

If data is outdated and irrelevant, the test automation suite might not be able to catch bugs. The near-production data (the data which is most similar to production data) ensures that the test data is mapped to the correct fields in the GUI. It should not contain leading and trailing spaces. Use test data with the correct spelling, since it may be relevant for selecting values from the drop-down menu, for example choosing data wisely for reuse across multiple tests. Test data is helpful in enhancing the code coverage. After a certain period the test data might become irrelevant; thus, it should be replaced by relevant and up-to-date test data to find bugs quickly and easily.

Investing in team building and training

Apart from the right tools and a well-laid process, a testing automation project requires a dedicated and skilled team to understand the complexity of the project and translate it into scripts. The gaps in the skillset imbalances the work and delivery, leading to patchwork and low morale of the team members. The leads or managers should see that the team gets adequate training to bridge the gaps (if any) in the skillset.

Conducting reviews and tests

Without formal reviews, it is likely that defects are not discovered and standards are not followed, leading to potential issues in the integration of framework components. This results in additional cost and effort. A review helps to proactively find issues and potential risks early and mitigate them quickly. Reviews also ensure consistency in the projects and keep the issues in check.

Summary

The automation life cycle is a structured approach to design, execute, and maintain test automation. This structured approach is necessary to help steer the test team away from common test program/automation mistakes.

This chapter covered all the aspects of test automation in a broader perspective. Having knowledge of the automation life cycle and key activities in each phase helps in streamlining tasks and goals. Well-defined processes and historical data are helpful in test estimation, and tool evaluation and selection. The architecture or design is based on implementing the test automation and achieving goals. In the next chapter, we will discuss the various features of QTP and concepts that are essential to create reusable scripts.

2
Essentials of Automation

In *Chapter 1, Automation Life Cycle and Automation Goals*, we learned about the test automation life cycle and automation goals. The basic features of the test automation are record and replay. These features allow the user to play scripts many times and compare expected values with actual values. This approach is simple and requires little or no knowledge of coding and can be applied to any supported application that has a graphical user interface. One should be familiar with basic QTP features, such as recording, replay, OR (Object Repository) creation, checkpoints, synchronization, actions, reporting, error handling, parameterization, and configuration. One should also know how to use environment variables to make the script complete and reusable. This chapter deals with recording or creating the test scripts, script creation life cycle, QTP features, and various ways of using these features to make complete reusable scripts. The intent of this chapter is not to gain in-depth knowledge but to get familiarized with these features for script creation and its enhancement.

About QTP

HP **QuickTest Professional** (**QTP** or QuickTest) or **Unified Functional Tester** (**UFT**) is the test automation tool for functional and regression test case automation. HP QuickTest Professional supports keyword view and scripting interfaces to automate the test. It uses VBScript as a scripting language to specify test scripts and working with the objects and controls in the application under test.

QTP is a tool that provides support for automated software testing and framework creation. The basic components that support QTP in recording and replay mechanism are test object model, test object, and object repository. The knowledge and understanding of these components is helpful in creating scripts.

The QuickTest object model

The test object model is a collection of objects and classes, which represents the objects in AUT. Each class has a set of properties for its identification; QTP uses a subset of the properties to identify the object uniquely at runtime.

Test script is a combination of standard VBScript statements and statements that use QuickTest test objects, methods, and properties. The QuickTest object model contains one section for each add-in environment available with the QTP installation, as well as a special section for utility and supplemental objects.

Test objects

QTP uses a test object to represent an object in AUT. Each test object has one or more methods and properties that are used to perform operations and retrieve values for that object. Each test object has a number of identification properties that describe the object.

Object identification properties can be used in the object repository description, programmatic descriptions, checkpoints, output values, test steps, and passed as argument values for `GetTOProperty` and `GetROProperty` methods. A runtime object is the actual object in AUT on which methods are performed during the run session.

Object repositories

Set up the resources before the test is created. One of the most important resources for any test is object repository, which stores the test objects (and other object types) used in your test. QuickTest can store the test objects it learns in two types of object repository files: shared and local.

A **shared object repository** contains test objects that can be used across multiple actions.

A **local object repository** stores test objects that can only be used in one specific action and not in any other action.

Record and replay

Recording is a process of capturing human actions performed on AUT and simultaneously creating a script, which can be replayed on AUT many times.

What happens when we record

When a user records the scripts, QTP perform various tasks as shown in following steps:

1. QTP uses a test object model. It identifies the test object and operation performed on an object that belongs to AUT.

2. Then it stores the test object in a local object repository on which the user performed the action.

3. Object identification properties of the test object are captured, which allows identification of the object uniquely at time of replay.

4. It provides a logical name to a test object, which makes objects' names readable.

5. Create a test step; a test step contains test objects including parent(s), operation, and data, if applicable. The following code is an example of the test step:

```
Dialog("Login").WinEdit("Agent Name:").Set "ashish"
```

In the previous test step, `Dialog` is the class name, `Login` is its logical name, and it is a parent of the `WinEdit` object. `WinEdit` is the class and `Set` is the operation, which sets the value as `ashish` to the object whose logical name is `Agent Name:`

The steps for recording are as follows:

1. Click on the **Record** button on the toolbar as shown in the following screenshot:

2. Perform the action on the AUT.

3. Repeat step 2 to record other test steps.

What happens when we replay

When QTP replays the scripts, it performs various tasks as shown in the following steps:

1. QTP finds the test object.

2. It identifies the test object uniquely; in some cases it may be using one of the following items: ordinal identifiers, smart identification, and relational identifiers.

3. Perform the intended operation on the runtime object.

The steps for recording are as follows:

Click on the **Run** button in the toolbar as shown in the following screenshot:

Script development

The steps for script development are as follows:

1. Analyze Application Under Test.
2. Create OR (add a test object manually).
3. Add test steps.
4. Enhance scripts by adding checkpoints, synchronization points, and so on.
5. Create a structure by inserting functions, actions, loops, and control statements.
6. Run and debug the test.
7. Analyze results and report defects.
8. Drag-and-drop object from OR to expert view.

We will discuss the preceding steps 4, 5, and 6 in later chapters.

Analyzing an application

Determine the development environment to load the relevant QuickTest add-ins and provide support for the objects in AUT. Analyze the flow and plan tests and actions accordingly. Decide the organization of the test, and ensure that the test and AUT are set to match the need of the automation.

Creating OR (adding test objects to OR)

When an object is added to an object repository, QuickTest performs the following actions:

1. It identifies the test object class, which represents the learned object and creates the appropriate test object.

2. It reads the current value of the object's properties in AUT as well as stores the list of identification properties. It selects the identification properties that can identify the test object uniquely.

3. It chooses a unique name for the test object, generally using the value of one of its prominent properties: for example, `name`, if the object has one.

Following are the ways to add the test object to OR:

1. Record a test step.
2. Add object to local.
3. Create an object description.
4. Create a test object by using define new test objects.
5. OR Manager Navigate and Learn or Add object option.
6. Adding test objects to the local object repository from **Active Screen**.

Recording a test step

Test objects are created automatically and added to the local OR when a user records a step. Add object to local.

Adding a test object to OR

Add a test object to the local OR through the following steps:

1. Navigate to **Resources | Object Repository | Add object to local**.
2. Click on the button **Add Object to local**.
3. Click on the hand pointer to the object we want to add from AUT.

4. Click on **OK**. The object is added to the OR as shown in the following screenshot:

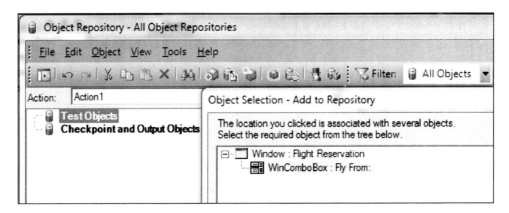

Creating an object description

The test object can be created without recording, by providing an object description. Refer to the following screenshot. The test object class name is `WinComboBox` and it has two description properties, which are stored with a logical name `Fly From:`

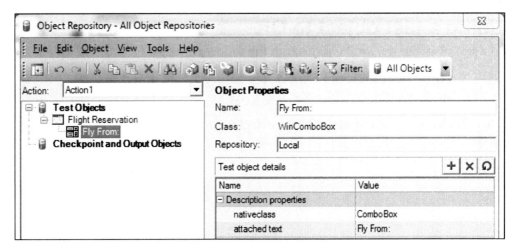

When we record the test step to select an option from the **Fly From** combobox, the following script is generated:

```
Window("FlghtReservation").WinComboBox("Fly From:").Select
    "London"
```

We can use the object description in the test steps directly, as shown in the following code:

```
Window("regexpwndtitle:=FlghtReservation").WinComboBox("attached
    text:=Fly From:").Select "London"
```

Both statements are the same when we replay the script, one uses an object from the OR and the other one uses the description directly. When we use programmatic description, the logical name is replaced by the pair(s) of the identification properties and its values.

Creating a test object using Define New Test Object

To define a new object, we should know its class and its identification properties. Perform the following steps:

1. Navigate to **Resources | Object Repository | Define New Test Object**.
2. Filter **Environment** from the **Define New Test Object** window.
3. Select the class from the **Class** drop-down box.
4. Enter a logical name.
5. Provide the value for the **Identification** property (1 to n).
6. If required, add some identification properties.
7. Click on the **Add** button to add a test object to the OR:

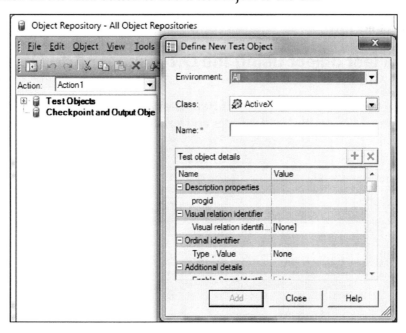

Select the environment displayed based on the loaded add-ins, select **Class**, and provide a logical name.

OR Manager Navigate and Learn and Add Object options

- How can I learn GUI Objects in one go?
- Use Navigate and Learn in the OR Manager.

The Navigate and Learn toolbar

This toolbar allows you to add multiple test objects to a shared object repository while you navigate through your application. Following are the steps to learn to navigate the object in the object repository manager:

1. Navigate to **Resources | Object Repository Manager | Object | Navigate and Learn** or press *F6*.

2. Select a window to learn. The selected window and its descendant objects are added to the active shared object repository according to a predefined object filter.

Adding a test object using the OR Manager Add Object option

1. Navigate to **Resources | Object Repository Manager | Objects | Add Object**. Click on the hand pointer and select the window.

2. The object filter is used for the **Navigate and Learn** option as well as the **Add Objects** option.

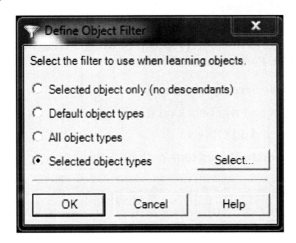

See the description of each filter in the following table:

UI Elements	Description
Selected object only (no descendants)	This option allows you to select objects without descendants and add the selected ones by previously using selected and its properties.
Default object types	This option enables adding selected objects and their descendants to the object repository. The objects selected are specified by the default filter option.
All object types	This option allows adding the objects and their descendants with properties and values selected previously in the object repository using the **Selected object typ**es option.
Selected object types	This option allows selecting and filtering the objects and their descendants. The selection remains valid until a user does not change the selection criteria.

Based on the filter option, the other is added to the OR.

Adding test objects to the local object repository from Active Screen

Select the required object from **Active Screen** and add it to the object repository. In order to add test objects to the object repository using **Active Screen, Active Screen** should have the object. Perform the following steps:

1. Go to the **Active Screen** pane.

2. Select an object and right-click on it.

3. Click on **View / Add Object**.

4. Click on the **Add to Repository** button.

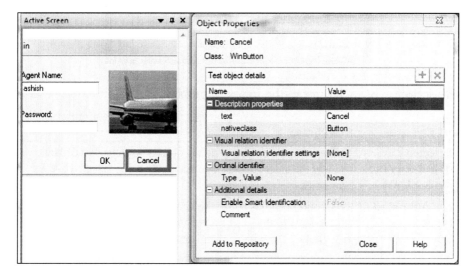

We have selected the object button **Cancel** as shown in the preceding screenshot. The test object is added to the local object repository and can be used only by the current action. We cannot add a test object in a shared OR (in OR Manager) using **Active Screen**.

Adding a test step

There are many ways in which we can add the steps in the scripts, as shown in the following steps:

- **Recording**: Recording creates the test step when a user performs the action on an object in AUT.

Manually adding a step: To add steps manually, we need to add the OR first. Write the class name, for example `Dialog`; the editor displays the list of dialogs. In case multiple dialogs are stored in OR, we can select the desired one. In case of a single dialog QTP, complete print the name of it in editor. When a user types `WinEdit`, the editor displays two objects that belong to the `WinEdit` class. Refer to the following screenshot:

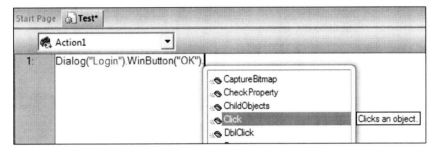

Press . on the keyboard after `WinButton("OK")`, the drop-down menu appears with the list of the methods available for the object. Select the appropriate method and complete the statement.

Perform the following steps for the keyword view:

1. Create the OR.
2. Switch to the keyword driven view.
3. Right-click on the **Item** column.
4. Select the object from the drop-down menu in the item of the grid.
5. Select the method from the **Operation** column.
6. Set the value, if required, in the **Value** column.

 The comment will be added by QTP itself.

If the test object is not added to the Object Repository before inserting the step, click on the object from the repository in the drop-down menu in the item column. Click on the hand pointer to add a test object from the repository in the selected test object window.

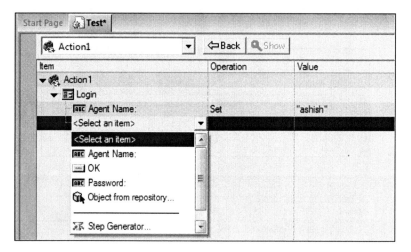

Step Generator from Keyword view:

1. Create the OR (add object to OR).
2. Switch to the keyword driven view and right-click on it.
3. Click on **Step Generator**.
4. Select **Test Object** from **Category**.
5. Select the test object from the dropdown or click on the icon (select the test object) to open the selected object window.
6. Select the test object.
7. Provide arguments and click on **OK**.

Adding steps to **Active screen**:

1. Open the **Active Screen** pane (if the **Active Screen** pan is not visible, go to **View | Active**).
2. Navigate to the object we want to add.
3. Click on the **Step Generator** option.
4. Select **Test Object** from **Category**.

5. Select the test object from the dropdown or click on the icon (select the test object) to open the selected object window.

6. Select the test object.

7. Provide the arguments.

Enhancing scripts

We have learned various ways of adding test objects and creating test steps, now we will learn about enhancing the scripts using checkpoints, actions, synchronization point, reporter object, Err handling, and environment variable to make it more reusable and effective.

Checkpoints

A checkpoint is a verification that compares the actual value for specified properties or the current state of other characteristics of an object with the expected value or characteristics. This allows notifying the **Run Result** window or scripts them as to whether applications are working as expected or not. When a checkpoint is added to the test, QuickTest inserts a checkpoint step in the keyword view and adds a `CheckPoint` statement in the expert view. When a test is executed, QuickTest compares the expected results and actual results using checkpoints. If there is a mismatch, the checkpoint fails. The results of the checkpoint can be viewed in the **Run Results Viewer**. See the various types of checkpoints in the following list:

Type	Description	How to insert	Example of use
Standard checkpoint	Verifies the value of an object's properties	Click on **Record** in toolbar. Navigate to **Insert	Checkpoint	Standard Checkpoint**.	Verify the property of the object
Image checkpoint	Verifies the properties of images	This checkpoint type is inserted by selecting the **Standard Checkpoint** option and then selecting to check a web image object.	Verify the `alt` property of the image

Type	Description	How to insert	Example of use
Table checkpoint	Verifies the information in the web table	This checkpoint type is inserted by selecting the **Standard Checkpoint** option and then selecting to check any table object.	Verify if the value of the cell in the web table is correct
Page checkpoint	Verifies the characteristics of a web page	This checkpoint type is inserted by selecting the Standard Checkpoint option and then selecting to check a web page object.	Verify the number of links
Text checkpoint	Verifies the displayed text or text within predefined and post-defined values	Click on **Record** in the toolbar. Navigate to **Insert | Checkpoint | Text Checkpoint**.	Verify if the expected text string is displayed
Text Area checkpoint	Verify if string is displayed within a defined area	Click on **Record** in the toolbar. Navigate to **Insert | Checkpoint | Text Area Checkpoint**.	Verify if the string defined in area matches with the expected string
Bitmap checkpoint	Verifies the bitmap or part of the bitmap	Click on **Record** in toolbar. Navigate to **Insert | Checkpoint | Bitmap Checkpoint**.	Check if bitmap matches the expected bitmap
Database checkpoint	Check if the value retrieved by query matches the expected value	Navigate to **Insert | Checkpoint | Database Checkpoint**.	Check if the value retrieved by query matches the expected value

Type	Description	How to insert	Example of use
Accessibility checkpoint	Identifies areas of a website to check for Section 508 compliancy	Click on **Record** in toolbar. Navigate to **Insert | Checkpoint | Accessibility Checkpoint**.	Check if the images on a web page include ALT properties, required by the W3C Web
XML checkpoint	Verifies data in XML documents	Navigate to **Insert | Checkpoint | XML Checkpoint**.	Check the value of an XML node and attributes

We will learn more about checkpoints in the next chapter.

Synchronization

When a test runs, it may not always match up to the speed of AUT and it is required to wait for the following. This is known as test synchronization.

- Wait until a progress bar reaches 100 percent
- Status message is displayed
- Wait until button is enabled
- Wait until a window or a pop up is displayed

In these scenarios, tests are either not able to perform the next step or synchronization times out, causing the test to fail. These issues can be resolved by various synchronization techniques provided by the QTP.

There are several options to synchronize a test with AUT:

1. Inserting the Wait statement allows a test to wait for a predefined time.
2. Insert a synchronization point or insert the WaitProperty method, allowing a test to pause until an object property achieves the specified value.
3. The Exist statement allows waiting until an object exists or times out.
4. QTP allows setting the default time-out for a web page to load.
5. Increase the default synchronization time-out by navigating to **File | Test | Run | object synchronization timeout**.

6. Use the `Sync` method for a web page to wait until the page is loaded. See the following code:

```
Browser("Mercury Tours").Page("Mercury Tours").Sync
```

 The synchronization point does not work when QTP is not able to identify the object; use `exist` or `wait` instead.

Exist statements

The `Exist` statement allows a test to wait for a window to open or an object to appear. `Exist` statements return a Boolean value indicating whether or not an object currently exists.

```
Done = Window("Flight Reservation").Dialog("Flights Table").Exist
Exitsinwaittime =Window("Flight Reservation").Dialog("Flights
   Table").Exist (10)
```

The first statement instructs QuickTest to wait until the default synchronization time. The second statement waits for a maximum of 10 seconds for the `Flights Table` dialog box to open.

 Downloading the example code

You can download the example code files for all Packt books you have purchased from your account at http://www.packtpub.com. If you purchased this book elsewhere, you can visit http://www.packtpub.com/support and register to have the files e-mailed directly to you.

Reporter objects

This object is used to send information to the run results. It has various methods and properties used at runtime to decide and change the control of flow of scripts. The following table demonstrates methods and properties of the reporter object.

Associated methods of the `Reporter` object	Associated properties of the `Reporter` **object**
`ReportEvent` method	`Filter` property
`ReportNote` method	`ReportPath` property
	`RunStatus` property

Let's see how to use these methods and properties:

It takes four arguments (`EventStatus`, `StepName`, `Details(Description)`, and `[, pathtosavefile]`) as shown in the following code:

```
Reporter.ReportEvent EventStatus, StepName, Details(Description)
   [,pathtosavethefile]
```

`EventStatus` is shown as a number or a constant. These constants are shown with the description of the message sent to the **Run Result** window as shown in the following table.

0 or micPass:	1 or micFail:	2 or micDone:	3 or micWarning:
Sends the passed message to the **Run Results** window	Sends the failed message to the **Run Results** window	Sends the message of doneness to the **Run Result** window	Sends a warning message to the **Run Results** window

The arguments list and its descriptions are mentioned in the following table:

Arguments	Type	Description
`ReportStepName`	`String`	Name of the step that the user wants to display in the **Run Results** window
`Details`	`String`	Sends the custom message or step description to run results
`ImageFilePath`	`String`	This argument is optional. The format to store the images are `.bmp`, `.jpeg`, `.png`, and `.gif` format

The following is the example of how to use the reporter object:

```
chk = Window("Flight Reservation").WinButton("FLIGHT").Check
   (CheckPoint("FLIGHT_2"))
if(chk = True) then
Reporter.ReportEvent micPass, "Verify Flight CheckPoint","Button
   is enabled"
else
'msgbox "Fail"
Reporter.ReportEvent micFail, "Verify Flight CheckPoint ","Button
   is disabled"
end if
```

The Reporter.RunStatus object

The `Reporter.RunStatus` object retrieves the current run status of the test. The following example demonstrates how to retrieve the value if it fails, and then exit from the test:

```
If Reporter.RunStatus = micFail Then ExitTest
```

This method also allows setting `RunStatus` as shown in the following code:

```
Reporter.RunStatus = micPass
```

Enable or disable the mode setting:

```
CurrentMode = Reporter.Filter To set the mode:  Reporter.Filter =
   NewMode
```

The mode can be one of the following values with description as shown in the following table:

Mode	Description
0 or `rfEnableAll` Default.	Displays all events in run results
1 or `rfEnableErrorsAndWarnings`	Displays the warning or fail status in run results
2 or `rfEnableErrorsOnly`	Displays the fail status in the run results
3 or `rfDisableAll`	Displays no events in run results

Actions

An action is a set of statements to perform a task(s); divide the test into actions to decompose the functionality into smaller and manageable scripts.

Purpose of actions

- Provide decomposition of scripts into manageable pieces
- Increase reusability

Types of actions

- **Non reusable actions**: They can be called in the same test only once and cannot be used in other tests.

- **Reusable actions**: Reusable actions can be used in the same test multiple times as well as in other tests.

- **External actions**: An external action is defined in another test and is used as read-only in calling a test and can be modified by a stored test.

Error handling

Error handling is an important aspect that allows coming up cleanly from erroneous conditions. QTP provides various options in case of an error.

Go to **File | Settings | Run | Select** when an error occurs during a run session; the options are:

- **Pop-up message box**: A pop-up message box displays the options selected by the user.

- **Proceed to the next test Iteration**: Skip the current iteration and move to the next one.

- **Stop Run**: Stop the test execution.

- **Proceed to the next step**: Skip the current step and proceed to the next one.

By specifying this action the test will come out of the error condition and proceed as a selected option. QTP also provides the recovery mechanism. Using VBScript we can handle various error situations using VBScript's ERR object. We will see how to use it in the later chapters of this book.

Parameterization

A parameter is a variable that holds a value(s). Parameterization allows substituting of values when a test is executed. QTP uses `datatable` to parameterize the test. Either a global or local sheet can be used for parameterization:

```
Dialog("Login").WinEdit("Agent Name:").Set DataTable("Name",
    dtGlobalSheet) 'Name is column name in datatable and retrieving
        the data from global sheet
```

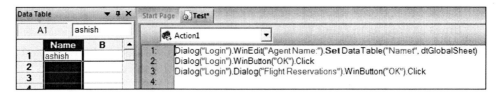

The data defined in `DataTable` or any external data source allows parameterizing of the test when a test is run for a number of rows in data sources. Parameterization helps to make the test iterative.

Environment Variables

QTP allows configuring of the test using environment variables. QTP provides built-in variables and allows the user to define variables as well. In-built environment variables can be viewed by navigating to **Test | Setting | Environment | Select Built-in** from the drop down.

The following example creates a new user-defined variable named `MyVariable` with a value of `15`, and then retrieves the variable value and stores it in the `MyValue` variable:

```
Environment.Value("MyVariable")=10
testvalue = Environment.Value("MyVariable")
```

We can create the `Environment` variable using XML as shown in the following code and add it by navigating to **Test | Setting | Environment | Select the user define option**. Set the export file from the load variable and XML from an external file. Use the **Browse** option to add it. The environment variable file must be an XML file; use the following syntax:

```
<Environment>
    <Variable>
        <Name>TestEnv</Name>
<!--  other environments are QA, Test and Dev -- >
        <Value>Staging</Value>
    </Variable>
</Environment>
```

QTP allows loading the specified environment variable file using the command
`Environment.LoadFromFile(Path)`.

The following example loads the `Environment.xml` file:

```
Environment.LoadFromFile("C:\Environment.xml")
'Check if an External Environment file is loaded and if not, load
   it.
fileName = Environment.ExternalFileName
If (fileName = "") Then
Environment.LoadFromFile("C:\Environment.xml")
End If
'display value of one of the Environment variables from the
   External file
msgbox Environment("TestEnv")
```

Summary

The key theme of this chapter was to learn how to create scripts and concepts that
are reliable and reusable. The smaller code examples demonstrate the usage of these
concepts. This chapter covered the steps required to create scripts and enhance
the scripts using checkpoints, parameterization, environment variables splitting
the actions, and adding the reporter object to notify the results in the **Run Result**
window. In the next chapter, the key discussion will be around building the key
features using code that can be utilized to develop the components that can be used
in frameworks.

3
Basic Building Blocks for Creating Frameworks

In the previous chapter, we have seen which QTP features are required to create scripts. To design a framework and its components we need to design reusable code blocks, apart from QTP features. The key features of code blocks are as follows:

- **Manual checkpoint**: This is a reusable function that checks whether the property is matching as expected at runtime

- **Manual synchronization**: This is a reusable function that waits up to a specified time for the property to change

- **Descriptive programming**: This provides the object identification property in test scripts to create the object description or creates the description itself

- **Regular expression**: This is a text string for matching a pattern and allows us to define objects that follow the pattern

- **Error handling with Err object and Exit statements**: Also known as exception handling, it guides us on how to come out of exceptional events and gracefully exit these conditions

- **Functions, subroutines, and procedures**: Functions and subprocedures allow us to make scripts modular and reusable

VBScript – key features for creating code blocks

VBScript is an easy-to-learn yet powerful scripting language. It is used to develop scripts to perform both simple and complex object-based tasks, even without previous programming experience. While working in the **Expert** view, use the following general VBScript syntax rules and guidelines:

- **Case sensitivity**: VBScript does not differentiate between uppercased and lowercased words. It is not case sensitive by default, for example, in constant, variable, object, and method names. The following two statements are identical:

```
Browser("Customer").page("Customer").weblist("date").select "31"
Browser("Customer").page("Customer").WebList("date").Select "31"
```

- **Text strings**: We can define a string by adding double quotes before and after the text string. In the following example, the string value is assigned using double quotes:

```
Dim objtype= "WinButton" or objtype= "WinButton"
```

  Date strings: We can define the date by adding hash marks before and after the date value; for example:

```
today = #7/10/2013#   or  Dim today = #7/10/2013#
```

- **Variables**: Variables are used to store strings, integers, dates, arrays, and objects. We can specify variables to refer to test objects or store simple values with or without using Dim. If used, the Option Explicit statement must appear in a script before any other statements. When the Option Explicit statement is declared, it forces us to explicitly declare variables using the Dim, Private, Public, or ReDim statements; otherwise, an error occurs.

  To specify a variable to refer to an object, use the Set statement with the following syntax:

```
Set ObjectVar = ObjectHierarchy
Set UserEditBox = Browser("email").Page("email").
WebEdit("username")
UserEditBox.Set "John"
```

Don't use the `Set` statement to specify a variable that contains a simple value (such as a string or number). The example that follows shows us how to define a variable for a simple value:

```
MyVar = Browser("email").Page("email").WebEdit("username").
GetTOProperty("text")
```
Or it can also be defined as:

```
Dim Myvar = Browser("email").Page("email").WebEdit("username").
GetTOProperty("text")
```

- **Comments**: Type `rem` or use an apostrophe (`'`) to add comments.
- **Spaces**: Spaces are ignored by VBScript; they just enhance the clarity and readability of the code.
- **Parentheses**: If the called function returns a value, use parentheses around the arguments.

The following example requires parentheses around the method arguments since it returns a value:

```
Set WebEditObj = Browser("Mercury").Page("Mercury").
WebTable("table").ChildItem (8, 2, "WebEdit", 0)
WebEditObj.Set "name"
```

The following example requires parentheses around method arguments, since **Call** is being used:

```
Call RunAction("BookFlight", oneIteration)
```

The following example requires parentheses around the method arguments since they return the value of the checkpoint:

```
result = Browser("Customer").Page("Customer").Check
(CheckPoint("MyProperty"))
```

The following example does not require parentheses around the `Click` method arguments since they don't return any values:

```
Browser("Mercury Tours").Page("Method of Payment").
WebTable("FirstName").Click
```

VBScript procedures

In VBScript, there are two types of procedures:

- Subprocedures
- Function procedures

Subprocedures

A subprocedure starts with the Sub statement and ends with the End Sub statement. Sub accepts arguments and does not return a value. An example is shown in the following code snippet:

```
Sub subSUM(a,b)
   print a+b
End Sub
```

Function procedures

A function procedure starts with the Function statement and ends with the End Function statement. It can return a value; the return value is always a variant. To return the value, assign it to the function name. An example of the function procedure is shown as follows:

```
Function funcSUM(a,b)
FuncSUM = a+b
End Function
```

Checkpoints

A checkpoint checks the specific values or characteristics of a page, object, or text string and enables the test object to identify whether the AUT is functioning correctly. A checkpoint compares the expected value (captured at the time of recording or creating the checkpoint) with the actual value (captured at runtime).

The following script creates the order using the Flight application; after selecting the FlyFrom insert checkpoint, we need to verify whether the **FLIGHT** button's **enabled** property is set to **True**:

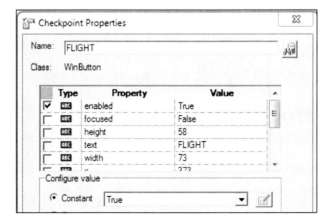

```
Window("WinFlight").Activate
Window("WinFlight").ActiveX("MaskEdBox").Type "111114"
Window("WinFlight").WinComboBox("FlyFrom:").Select "Frankfurt"
'Insert a checkpoint to verify if button is enabled or not
Window("WinFlight").WinButton("FLIGHT").Check CheckPoint("WINFLIGHT")
'In the preceding checkpoint verify if button is enabled or not
isChkPointPass= Window("WinFlight").WinButton("FLIGHT").Check
(CheckPoint("FLIGHT"))
'Note: We have used the bracket around Checkpoint to get the outcome
If isChkPointPass = True Then
   'Continue with order of creation
   Window("WinFlight").WinComboBox("FlyTo:").Select "Paris"
Window("WinFlight").WinButton("FLIGHT").Click
Window("WinFlight").Dialog("FlightsTable").WinButton("WinOK").Click
Window("WinFlight").WinEdit("Name:").Set "ashish"
Window("WinFlight").WinButton("Insert Order").Click
   Else
       'Leave the action if a checkpoint fails
   ExitAction
End If
```

Output value

An **output value** is a value that is retrieved during the test execution from DataTable or saved in a variable or parameter. When the output value is executed, the Output method places the object's property value into the prespecified column (which is defined when the test was created) and is retrieved through the DataTable. Later, this value is used to verify the expected and actual value; thus, we can use the output value as a checkpoint.

The following code snippet creates a checkpoint using the output values:

```
Window("WinFlight").Activate
Window("WinFlight").ActiveX("MaskEdBox").Type "111114"
Window("WinFlight").WinComboBox("FlyFrom:").Select "Frankfurt"
'Insert an output value to verify if button is enabled or not
Window("WinFlight").WinButton("FLIGHT"). Output CheckPoint("FLIGHT")
'The first column represents from where value is retrieved and the
second column represents sheet Global/local
outval= Datatable("WINFLIGHT_Button",dtGlobalSheet)
'Verify the expected and actual values and report them in test results
using reporter.reportevent
If   outval = True Then
```

```
Reporter.ReportEvent micPass,"Verify WinFlight Button", "Match"
else
Reporter.ReportEvent micFail,"Verify WinFlight Button", "The
property value does not match with the expected value"
ExitAction
End If
```

We can create a manual checkpoint using the `CheckProperty` method as well. `CheckProperty` allows us to use various options, and we can check the not equal condition as well.

How to check an equal condition using `CheckProperty`:

```
Window("WinFlight").WinButton("FLIGHT").CheckProperty( "enabled",
True, 10000)
```

Checkpoints allow the following options to ascertain various unequal options:

- `micGreaterThan`: This option verifies whether the value of the property is greater than the expected value.

- `micLessThan`: This option verifies whether the value of the property is less than the expected value.

- `micGreaterThanOrEqual`: This option verifies whether the value of the property is greater than or equal to the expected value.

- `micLessThanOrEqual`: This option verifies whether the value of the property is less than or equal to the expected value.

- `micNotEqual`: This option verifies whether the value of the property is not equal to the expected value.

  The following example demonstrates how to use the not equal option:

  ```
  Window("WinFlight").WinComboBox("FlyTo:").CheckProperty("items
  count", micGreaterThanOrEqual(10), 10000)
  ```

- `micRegExpMatch`: The `CheckProperty` also allows us to use regular expressions. The `micRegExpMatch` option verifies if the property value matches with the regular expression, as shown in the following example, and how to use the regular expression with `CheckProperty`:

  ```
  Window("WinFlight").WinEdit("Order No:").CheckProperty ("text",mic
  RegExpMatch("\d{1,3}"),10000)
  Creating checkpoint using GetROProperty
  ```

GetROProperty returns the current value of the specified identification property from the runtime object in the AUT. We can use the GetROProperty to create the checkpoint. Using this checkpoint, we will get the runtime property, and we can compare it with the expected value as shown in the following example:

```
Required. A String value. Property to retrieve from the object.
Required. A String value. Property to retrieve from the object.
'We are retrieving the value of enable property of the FLIGHT
Button and comparing it with expected value thus serves as a check
to take a further action
Pvalue =Window("WinFlight").WinButton("FLIGHT").
GetRoProperty("enabled")
If Pvalue = True Then
  'Create the order
  Else
'Exit the Test
  ExitTest
End If
```

When we design the framework and its components, we need to create manual checkpoints for reusability; a good practice is to create them as reusable functions.

Synchronization

QTP and AUT join or handshake at a certain point to match up their speeds for the event to occur in order to accomplish a certain sequence of action.

Speed mismatch, delays, the wait for property to change, change of object, and occurrence of an event causes mismatch in the speed of execution of scripts, and AUT causes synchronization issues, for example, script has to wait until the page is loaded. The default object synchronization is 20 seconds but we can change it by navigating to **File | Test Settings | Run | Object synchronization timeout**.

Change the **Object synchronization timeout** from **20** seconds to **2** seconds as shown in the following screenshot:

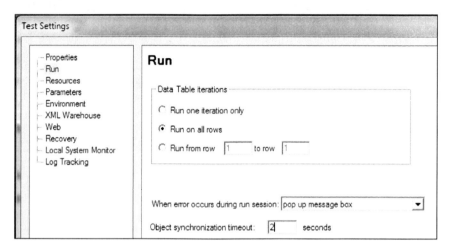

Now that we have changed the **Object synchronization timeout** value, we will run the following script:

```
'Open the Flight Reservation login window and create the script
Dialog("DialogLogin").WinEdit("AgentName").Set "ashish"
Dialog("DialogLogin").WinEdit("AgentPassword").SetSecure
"51d84ff2108dc473a416b19e1fed478fab95ca75"
Dialog("DialogLogin").WinButton("WinOK").Click
'The script will fail at this step, the object synchronization is 2
seconds but window takes more time to open; hence script fails
Window("WinFlight").Activate
```

To achieve synchronization, we introduce some wait scripts that wait for the specified time. Refer to the following code snippet:

```
Dialog("DialogLogin").Activate
Dialog("DialogLogin").WinEdit("AgentName").Set "ashish"
Dialog("DialogLogin").WinEdit("AgentPassword").SetSecure
"51d84ff2108dc473a416b19e1fed478fab95ca75"
Dialog("DialogLogin").WinButton("WinOK").Click
'The script will fail at this step. To avoid this, insert a wait
statement
wait 10'Window("WinFlight").Activate
```

The `wait` statement tells QTP to wait for a predefined amount of time, for example, 10 seconds. Here, the following situations can arise:

- The AUT is ready to perform the next step, but the script is still waiting till the specified time
- The wait time is over and the AUT is still not ready for the next step to be executed

In both of these conditions, static wait is not a good option. Waiting for an appropriate amount of time based on some property or event that has to be completed is called dynamic synchronization.

Dynamic synchronization

Dynamic synchronization allows waiting till the object property is changed or till time out, as shown in the following example:

```
Window("WinFlight").ActiveX("MaskEdBox").Type "111114"
Window("WinFlight").WinComboBox("FlyFrom:").Select "Frankfurt"
Window("WinFlight").WinComboBox("FlyTo:").Select "Los Angeles"
Window("WinFlight").WinButton("FLIGHT").Click
Window("WinFlight").Dialog("FlightsTable").WinButton("WinOK").Click
Window("WinFlight").WinEdit("Name:").Set "ashish"
Window("WinFlight").WinButton("Insert Order").Click
'Window("WinFlight").WinButton("Button").Click
'When QTP tries to execute the following statement, application will
not allow to click on the button since it is waiting for progress bar
to reach 100% and display the message Insert Done...
'Here script will fail
'We need  to insert the dynamic synchronization point; this waits
until the text changes to Insert Done...
'Window("WinFlight").ActiveX("ThreedPanelControl").WaitProperty
"text", "Insert Done...", 10000
```

The `WaitProperty` can be inserted using Insert synchronization point or we can manually add the `WaitProperty` method by typing it.

Apart from using `WaitProperty`, we can also create synchronization points using the following code:

```
Set Object = Window("WinFlight").ActiveX("ThreedPanelControl")
Set WinsObject = Window("WinFlight")
'It accepts the object with its property and value. You have to wait
along with timeout
```

```
Function ManualSyncPoint (Object,propertyname, propertyval,timeout )
    Do
    If Object.GetROProperty(propertyname)   =propertyval then
'if propertyname and propertyval match, come out of the loop and
execute next step
        Exit Do
    else
        wait(1)
end if
    Loop While (i <= timeout)
End Function
'In the preceding method we have used the static wait; we can
implement it without using wait statement as well
Example 2:
Function ManualSyncPoint2(Object ,propertyname, propertyval, timeout )
    sttimer = Timer
'Timer allows to get the number of seconds elapsed since midnight
(12:00 AM)
    Do
    If Object.GetROProperty(propertyname)   = propertyval then
Exit Do
    else
        end if
          endtimer = Timer
     'The difference between the two timer objects provides the number
of seconds we need to determine for timeout
    Loop While ( int (endtimer-sttimer) <= -timeout)
 End Function
'Function that allows to wait till object exists
Function WaitTillExists(Object, timeout )
loadtimer = Timer
 Do
        isObjectExists = Object.Exist
   If isObjectExists = true Then
   Exit Do
     else
   End If
     completetimer = Timer
 Loop While(completetimer-loadtimer  <= timeout)
End Function
'Now we will use these functions in our scripts; refer to the
following script
Dialog("DialogLogin").Activate
Dialog("DialogLogin").WinEdit("AgentName").Set "ashish"
```

```
Dialog("DialogLogin").WinEdit("Password").SetSecure
"51d84ff2108dc473a416b19e1fed478fab95ca75"
Dialog("DialogLogin").WinButton("WinOK").Click
' wait
'Go to the test settings and make object synchronization time to 2 sec
WaitTillExists WinsObject, 10
Window("WinFlight").Activate
Window("WinFlight").ActiveX("MaskEdBox").Type "111114"
Window("WinFlight").WinComboBox("FlyFrom:").Select "Frankfurt"
Window("WinFlight").WinComboBox("FlyTo:").Select "Los Angeles"
Window("WinFlight").WinButton("FLIGHT").Click
Window("WinFlight").Dialog("FlightsTable").WinButton("WinOK").Click
Window("WinFlight").WinEdit("Name:").Set "ashish"
Window("WinFlight").WinButton("Insert Order").Click
Window("WinFlight").WinButton("Button").Click
'When QTP tries to execute the following statement, the application
will not allow to click on the button since it is waiting for progress
bar to reach 100% and display the message Insert Done...
'Here script will fail
'We need to insert the dynamic synchronization point
Window("WinFlight").ActiveX("ThreedPanelControl").WaitProperty "text",
"Insert Done...", 5000

'The preceding statement waits till the text property changes to
Insert Done... and waits for upto 10 secs
 If ManualSyncPoint1(Object ,"text","Insert Done…",10)  = true then
   'do nothing
  else
  ExitTest
  end if
Window("WinFlight").WinButton("Button").Click
```

Descriptive programming

QTP identifies an object by its properties that are stored in the OR. When the object description is created in the test script, the approach is called descriptive programming. In this method of script creation, objects are not stored in the OR.

Descriptive programming can be achieved in two ways:

- **Static programming**: The object's description is directly provided into the script

- **Dynamic programming**: The object's description is created using QTP's description object

Static programming

Examples of static descriptive programming are shown as follows:

```
'Add object description as property value pair
Dialog("regexpwndclass:=Login").Activate
Dialog("regexpwndclass:=Login").WinEdit("regexpwndclass:=Edit","attach
ed text:=AgentName").Set "ashish"
Dialog("regexpwndclass:=Login").WinEdit("regexpwndclass:=Edit","attach
ed text:=AgentPassword").Set "mercury"
Dialog("regexpwndclass:=Login").WinButton("regexpwndtitle:=OK").Click
'The multiple property and value pair is provided in the object
description; property value pair should be comma separated

Method 2: Define Description as constant
Note:
Constant represents the literal value and gives it a name that is not
allowed to change at time of script execution. Declare constants for
use in place of literal values. For example, Const Env = "QA"
Define Constant
Name of the constant and expression; expression is Literal or another
constant, or any combination that includes all arithmetic or logical
operators
Constant can be declared as Public or Private. A variable that is
declared as a constant is available to all procedures in all scripts.
Not allowed in procedures. The Private keyword is used at script
level to declare constants available only within the script where the
declaration is made. Not allowed in procedures
Const Dailoglogin ="regexpwndtitle:=Login"
Const agent = "attached text:=AgentName"
Const password = "attached text:=Password:"
Const okButton ="text:=OK"

Dialog(Dialoglogin).Activate
Dialog(Dialoglogin).WinEdit(agent).Set "ashish"
Dialog(Dialoglogin).WinButton(okButton).Click

Method 3: Substitution of property values shown as follows

dialogname ="login"
agentname ="AgentName"
passwdname ="Password:"
buttonlabel="OK"

Dialog("regexpwndtitle:="&dialogname).Activate
```

```
Dialog("regexpwndtitle:="&dialogname).WinEdit("attached
text:="&agentname).Set "ashish"
Dialog("regexpwndtitle:="&dialogname).WinEdit("attached
text:="&passwdname).Set "mercury"
Dialog("regexpwndtitle:="&dialogname).WinButton("text:="&
buttonlabel).Click
```

Dynamic programming

QTP allows the use of the Description object and its Create method to create the object description and pass it as an argument to create the scripts.

The following is an example of the same:

```
Set diaDesc = Description.Create()
diaDesc("micclass").value="Dialog"
diaDesc("regexpwndtitle").Value ="Login"

Set btnDesc=Description.Create()
btnDesc("micclass").value="WinButton"
btnDesc("text").value="OK"

Set txtDesc = Description.Create()
txtDesc("micclass").value="WinEdit"
txtDesc("attached text").Value ="AgentName"

Set pwdDesc = Description.Create()
pwdDesc("micclass").value="WinEdit"
pwdDesc("attached text").Value ="Password:"

'Use these objects into the scripts shown as follows

Dialog(diaDesc).Activate
Dialog(diaDesc).WinEdit(txtDesc).Set "ashish"
Dialog(diaDesc).WinEdit(pwdDesc).Set "mercury"
Dialog(diaDesc).WinButton(btnDesc).Click
```

The test objects that have the same identification properties are called **duplicate objects**. Ordinal identifiers allow us to identify duplicate objects using the `index` and `location` properties. `index` represents the order of the objects from left to right and top to bottom. `location` represents the objects from top-left to bottom and top-right to bottom.

```
'Ordinal Identifier stats with 0
Browser("email").Page("email").WebEdit("name:=FNAME", "index:=0").Set
"Ashish1"
Browser("email").Page("email").WebEdit("name:=FNAME", "index:=1").Set
"Ashish2"
Browser("email").Page("email").WebEdit("name:=FNAME", "index:=2").Set
"Ashish3"
Browser("email").Page("email").WebEdit("name:=FNAME", "index:=3").Set
"Ashish4"
```

The outcome after we run the script is as follows:

```
Browser("email").Page("email").WebEdit("name:=FNAME", "location:=0").
Set "Ashish1"
Browser("email").Page("email").WebEdit("name:=FNAME", "location:=1").
Set "Ashish2"
Browser("email").Page("email").WebEdit("name:=FNAME", "location:=2").
Set "Ashish3"
Browser("email").Page("email").WebEdit("name:=FNAME", "location:=3").
Set "Ashish4"
The outcome after we run the script is as follows
```

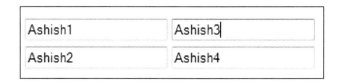

Descriptive programming allows us to deal with dynamic objects; this is a situation where the test object does not exist till runtime, so we cannot store the dynamic objects in the OR. For example, a textbox is generated based on the user ID in the web page at runtime and the name of the object follows the convention edit_xxx, that is, edit_123455.

The code is provided on the preceding page; now we will write the code to set the value as shown in the following code snippet:

```
Code = getCode() ' getCode is a function that's return the code
given in previous page, we can use that code to create the object
description for webEdit
Browser("email").Page("email").WebEdit("name:=text_"&Code).Set "jonh"
```

One use of descriptive programming is that it allows us to find the object(s) at runtime and performs the following operations on it/them:

```
Set buttonDesc=Description.Create()
buttonDesc("micclass").value="WinButton"
Set winAll=Window("regexpwndtitle:=Flight Reservation").
ChildObjects(buttonDesc)
cnt=winAll.count
MsgBox "Total number of Buttons: "&cnt
For i=0 to cnt-1
  MsgBox winAll(i).getroproperty("text")
   If  winAll(i).Getroproperty("text")="FLIGHT" Then
  winAll(i).Click
    End If
Next
```

Regular expressions

A regular expression (abbreviated regex or regexp) is a sequence of text characters, some of which are understood to be meta characters with symbolic meaning and some of which have their literal meaning, that together automatically identify a given pattern.

A regular expression is very useful when the objects are dynamic in nature and we cannot store each and every object which follows a pattern in the OR. In the Flight Reservation application, we can open any existing order by the order number and send the fax. When the **Fax** window is opened, the title of the window contains the order number; this will cause an issue when we want to open the fax window with a different order number as the window is no longer the same. In this condition, we can use regular expression. Refer to the following screenshot; the identification property of the object is **Fax Order No. 11**. Here we convert the **text** property into a regular expression to identify the property as a pattern and not a fixed value.

The regular expression shown in the following screenshot matches a pattern where the number of digits may vary from **1** to **3**. This means that it is used to verify the **Fax** window title from 0 to 999.

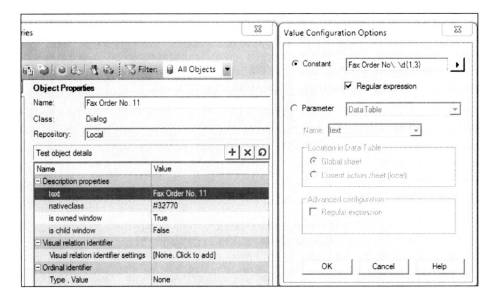

Regular expressions in descriptive programming

In the earlier screenshot, we have seen that once we change the **text** property to the regular expression, QTP is able to identify objects with order numbers from 0 to 999. We can use the regular expression in object description as shown in the following code:

```
Window("WinFlight").Dialog("regexpwndclass:=#32770", "text:=Fax Order
No\. \d{1,3}").Activex("progid:=MSMask.MaskEdBox.1").Type "1111111111"
```

Regular expressions in checkpoints

A checkpoint allows us to use the regular expression for matching the pattern. To use the regular expression in a checkpoint, do the following:

1. Click on **Parameter Options** in the **Text Checkpoint Properties** window.
2. Click on 📝.
3. Check the **Regular expression** option in **Parameter Options**.

4. Click on **OK** and change the parameter to regular expressions (in **DataTable**) as shown in the following screenshot.

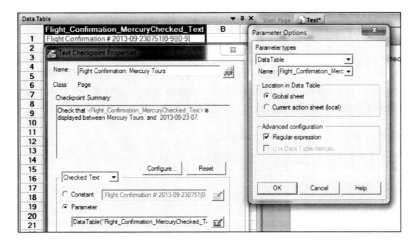

Regular expressions in CheckProperty

CheckProperty allows us to compare the values using regular expressions and micRegExpMatch as shown in the following code snippet:

```
'Verify whether the order number is numeric
Window("WinFlight").WinEdit("Order No:").CheckProperty ("text",micRegE
xpMatch("\d{1,3}"),10000)
```

Error handling

Exception handling is the way to deal with abnormal or exceptional events that interrupt the normal flow of test execution. For example, when a floating point number is divided by zero (0), it stops execution and an error message is displayed as shown in the following piece of code:

```
Type in the QTP editor
Result = 5 / 0
'When test runs the preceding line, it will display Error Division by
zero
```

The Err object in VBScript holds the details of the runtime errors, allowing continued execution despite a runtime error.

If the `On Error Resume Next` statement is absent in the script, any runtime error will stop execution and display the error message as shown:

```
On Error Resume Next
Result = 5 / 0
'The above line will not display any error
```

Using the `On Error Resume Next` statement allows us to continue with the exception, but it is necessary to deal with the error using the `Err` object and come out clean from the erroneous condition.

The properties of the `Err` object are as follows:

- `Description` property
- `HelpContext` property
- `HelpFile` property
- `Number` property
- `Source` property

The methods of the `Err` object are as follows:

- `Clear` method
- `Raise` method

```
On Error Resume Next 'Enables the Err object to deal with error
'Raise an overflow error.
Err.Raise 6
MsgBox "Error number is" & CStr(Err.Number) & "--" & Cstr(Err.
Description))
'Clear the error.
Err.Clear
```

Use `On Error GoTo 0` to disable error handling if `On Error Resume Next` has been used.

Examples are shown in the following code snippet of how to use the `Err` object for error handling:

```
On Error Resume Next
Const ForReading = 1
Dim fso, theFile, retstring
   Set fileso = CreateObject("Scripting.FileSystemObject")
   Set theFile = fileso.OpenTextFile("c:\FilenotFound.txt",
ForReading)
```

```
'Verify if error number of the Err object using its property number
   If Err.number <> 0 then
   'Error send there is no file exists by FilenotFound.txt
  MsgBox Cstr(Err.number & "--"&  Cstr(Err.Description)
   ExitAction(-1)
else
  'Do While   theFile.AtEndOfStream <> True
Do until   theFile.AtEndOfStream
     str = theFile.ReadLine()
     MsgBox str
  Loop
   theFile.Close
   end if
```

The Exit statements in QTP are very important; they allow us to gracefully exit from loops, actions, iterations, components, and tests.

The different types of Exit statements are shown as follows:

- Exit Do: This statement allows us to exit a Do loop statement.

- Exit For: This statement allows us to exit a For loop.

- Exit Function: This statement allows us to exit the Function procedure in which it is called.

- Exit Property: This statement allows us to exit the Property procedure.

- Exit Sub: This allows statement us to exit the Sub procedure in which it is called.

- ExitAction: This statement allows us to exit from the current iteration of an action.

- ExitTest: This statement allows us to exit the entire QTP or **Quality Centre (QC)** business process test, regardless of the runtime iteration settings.

- ExitTestIteration: This statement allows us to exit the test iteration or QC's business process test and moves on to the next iteration. If there is no next iteration, it stops execution.

The return value of ExitActionIteration is displayed in the **Run Result** window.

- ExitComponent: This statement allows us to exit the current component run.

  In **Business Process Testing (BPT)**, each component (scripted or business) is the same as a QTP Test with a single action. A business process runs each component one by one. QC loads the component in QTP and starts the run. Once the run is complete, the next component in the test is loaded, and all the results are collated into a single test result summary.

- `ExitComponentIteration`: This statement allows us to exit the current component iteration.

The following example demonstrates the use of the `Exit` statement(s) if the checkpoint fails:

```
res = Browser("Mercury").Page("Mercury").WebEdit("userName").Check (
CheckPoint("Name") )
If res = False Then
'ExitActionIteration /ExitAction / /ExitTestIteration /ExitTest /
ExitComponentIteration /ExitComponent
'We can use any one of them to gracefully exit based on how test is
executing.
End If
```

Recovery scenarios – an overview

Any unexpected event or erroneous condition that crashes the AUT during execution needs to be recovered. To handle these situations, QTP allows us to define the recovery scenarios and associates them with the test. Recovery scenarios activate specific recovery operations when trigger events occur.

The recovery scenario manager allows us to define the recovery scenario, that includes an unexpected event and the operations to recover during a run session. For example, an unexpected pop-up message appears and the recovery scenario is recovered from it by clicking on the **OK** button in the pop up.

A recovery scenario has the following elements:

- **Trigger event**: Any event that abruptly interferes with the normal flow of the test runs, for example, a dialog pops up during test execution.

- **Recovery operations**: The recovery option allows QTP to continue running the test or its components after the trigger event hampers test execution. For example, closing the pop-up window or a call to restart the window.

- **Post-recovery option**: QTP provide options after the recovery operations have been executed, for example, calling a custom function, executing the same step, or executing the next step in the test or component.

After recovery scenarios are created, we can associate them with selected components/tests. So, QTP will perform the appropriate scenarios during the run sessions if a trigger event occurs.

Summary

In this chapter we have gone through various concepts and code blocks. The key is to understand that apart from the QTP features, we need other components that support the entire design and architecture of the framework. One of the key aspects for creating code blocks is to enhance the reusability and create an impact on every feature of designing the framework. The next chapter will talk about designing and implementing the test automation framework.

4

Understanding and Creating Frameworks

This chapter provides a detailed approach and guidance for creating a framework for test automation.

Creating frameworks in QTP requires knowledge of the following:

- VBScript basics, control structures, loops, and built-in functions
- Basic concepts and approaches for designing various frameworks
- Programming constructs that help to create the utilities for the framework

Programming with VBScript

Knowledge of Visual Basic script is essential to create frameworks. The knowledge of creating simple statements, controls structure, loops, and built-in functions in VBScript allows us to enhance the test scripts and make them more robust; it also allows us to interact with external resources. This section describes the VBScript features that are useful throughout the designing of the frameworks.

Using VBScript

QTP uses VBScript as a scripting language. VBScript allows scripts to deal with resources that are not a part of the QTP itself, for example, filesystem and external data sources (Excel, databases, and so on). VBScript allows us to define the function procedures; it provides a lot of built-in functions that help to create the reusable functions. VBScript supports the regular expression that assists in verification and validation. Since it's a lightweight language, the framework designer is benefited.

VBScript datatypes

Variant is the only datatype in VBScript. A variant can contain different kinds of information depending on its declaration and use. It can contain numeric, constant, date, string, and Boolean values.

The following is a list of the subtypes of a variant:

Subtype	Description	Range
Empty	Variant is uninitialized	0 for the numeric variables
		"" or Zero-length for the string variables
Null	Variant initially contains no valid data	Does not contain data
Boolean		True or False
Byte	Small integer	0-255
Integer	Integer	From -32,768 to 32,767
Currency	Currency	From -922,337,203,685,477.5808 to 922,337,203,685,477.5807
Long	Long integer	From -2,147,483,648 to 2,147,483,647
Single	Single-precision floating-point number	From -3.402823E38 to -1.401298E-45 for negative values, and from 1.401298E-45 to 3.402823E38 for positive values
Double	Double-precision floating-point number	1.79769313486232E308 to 4.94065645841247E-324 for negative values, and 4.94065645841247E-324 to 1.79769313486232E308 for positive values
Date (Time)	A number that represents a date	Dates from January 1, 100 to December 31, 9999
String	Represents the characters	Contains characters of variable length string, approximately 2 billion in length
Object	Contains an object	
Error	Contains an Error object	

Operators in VBScript

Operators are useful in creating the expressions; these expressions are created by arithmetic, comparison, and logical operators. In VBScript, we can divide operators into four major categories:

- Mathematical
- Comparison
- Concatenation
- Logical

Mathematical	Symbol	Comparison	Symbol	Logical	Symbol
Exponential	^	Equality	=	Logical negation	Not
Urinary negation	-	Inequality	<>	Logical conjunction	And
Multiplication	*	Less than	<	Logical disjunction	OR
Division	/	Greater than	>	Logical exclusion	XOR
Integer division	\	Less than equal to	<=	Logical equivalence	EQV
Modulus	MOD	Greater than equal to	>=	Logical implication	IMP
Addition	+	Object equivalence**	Is		
Subtraction	-				
Concatenation	&				

Integer division divides two numbers and returns an integer result, for example, 5/2 will result in 2 not 2.5.

The modulus or remainder operator divides operand 1 by operand 2 (rounding the floating-point number to an integer) and returns a remainder, for example, 5 MOD 2 will result in 1.

Object equivalence compares two object reference variables. If object1 and object2 both refer to the same object, the result is True; if they don't, the result is False.

Adding examples of expressions

An expression is a combination of explicit values, constants, variables, operators, and functions that are interpreted according to particular rules of precedence and association for a particular programming/scripting language.

Control structures and loops

A control structure, conditionally, executes a group of statements, depending on the value of an expression. There are four constructs that control the flow of the execution, which are shown in the following table:

If (condition) statement1 End If	If condition Then statements [Else else statements] End If	If condition Then [statements] [ElseIf condition Then [elseif statements]] [Else [else statements]] End If	Select Case expression [Case expression list [statements]] [Case Else [else statements]] End Select

An example of the `If` and `else` control statement is given as follows:

```
If True Then
Reporter.ReportEvent micPass,"Name of the step", "Details..."
Else
Reporter.ReportEvent micFail, "Name of the step", "Details..."
End If
If elseif … and end if
color ="b"

If color ="r" Then
   msgbox "red"
  elseif  color ="g" then
  msgbox "green"
  elseif color="b" then
  msgbox "blue"
  else
  msgbox "invalid color..."
End If
```

The following is an example of the `Select` case:

```
Dim Color, bgcolor
    Select Case Color
        Case "red"      bgColor = "red"
        Case "green"    bgColor = "green"
        Case "blue"     bgColor = "blue"
        Case Else       MsgBox "pick another color"
    End select
    Msgbox "You have Selected the "& bgcolor
```

Running the preceding lines of code executes a series of statements as long as the given condition is `True`.

Using loops

A loop executes a sequence of statements that are specified once but may be carried out several times in succession. VBScript allows four looping constructs as shown in the following table:

While ... Wend	Do... Loop	For... Next	For each... Next
While condition	Do [{While | Until} condition]	For counter = start To end [Step step]	For each element in collection
[statements]	[statements]	[statements]	[statements]
Wend	[Exit Do]	[Exit For]	[Exit For]
	[statements]	[statements]	[statements]
	Loop	Next	Next [element]
	Do		
	[statements]		
	[Exit Do]		
	[statements]		
	Loop [{While | Until} condition]		

The following is an example of the usage of `While ... Wend`:

```
'Print 10 random numbers
counter = 0 'Initialize the counter
While counter < 10
  print Cint( rnd() * 100 )
  counter = counter + 1 'Increment the counter
Wend
```

One of the drawbacks of the `While...Wend` loop is that it does not have the `exit` statement to terminate from the loop but other looping constructs allow us to exit from the loop.

The Do Loop

The `Do...Loop` runs statements for an indefinite number of times. The statements are repeated either while a condition is true or until it becomes true.

The following is an example of the usage of `Do Loops`:

```
'Execute the loop until the response until CANCEL button is clicked
Usages 1
Do Until DefResp = vbNo
    MyNum = Int (6 * Rnd + 1)
  'Generate a random number between 1 and 6.
    DefResp = MsgBox (MyNum & "Do you want another number?", vbYesNo)
'The msgbox displays generated random number and OK and Cancel button
Loop
Usages 2
Do while not DefResp = vbNo
    MyNum = Int (6 * Rnd + 1)
    DefResp = MsgBox (MyNum & "Do you want another number?", vbYesNo)
Loop
Usages 3
Do
    MyNum = Int (6 * Rnd + 1)
    DefResp = MsgBox (MyNum & "Do you want another number?", vbYesNo)
Loop until DefResp = vbNo
```

There are two variants of `Do Loop`; we can use the `while` or `until` conditions with `Do` or `Loop`. When we use the `while` or `until` condition with `Do`, the execution starts with validating the condition first and then enters into the loop; refer to example 1. In the latter case, example 3, the first loop is executed once and the condition is checked later.

The `For Next` loop iterates statements over a predefined number of times. Refer to the following code.

The `ToProperties` method returns a collection of the properties of the test object.

```
set Pcoll =
Dialog("DialogLogin").WinEdit("EditAgentName:").GetTOProperties()
```

```
For i = 0 to coll.count() - 1
'Count method return the numbers of properties
  -print "Item is  " & Pcoll.item(i)
Next
```

The result of the preceding set of code is as follows:

```
Item is Edit
Item is Agent Name:
Refer the above results and compare the properties of the object
  are same in the following image.
```

Refer to the following screenshot:

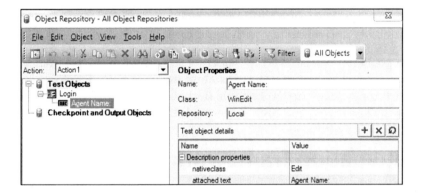

The `For each ... Next` loop iterates statements for each element in an array or collection.

`Dim dicObj` creates a dictionary variable, which is shown as follows:

```
Set city = CreateObject("Scripting.Dictionary") 'Creates
  Dictionary Object
'Dictionary stores data key, item (key - value) pairs.
'Add keys and items.
dicObj.Add "a", "Atlanta"
dicObj.Add "b", "Paris"
dicObj.Add "c", "New Delhi"
'Keys is a method that returns an array or collection containing
  all existing keys in a Dictionary object.
For each keyitem in d.Keys
    print keyitem
Next
```

Introducing frameworks

A framework is defined as a broad overview, guideline, or skeleton of the interlinked components, which supports a particular approach to a specific objective, and serves as a guide that can be enhanced as required by adding or deleting components. A framework is a working or conceptual model that supports or provides guidelines for creating or expanding the test scripts to achieve the test automation, ensuring lower maintenance and easy expandability.

A test automation framework is a layered structure and provides the mechanism to interrelate and interact with each other to achieve the common goals. Frameworks also include actual programs and interfaces or offer utility tools for using the frameworks. A framework facilitates a standard way for modifying, adding, and deleting the scripts and functions. It's a comprehensive structure that provides scalability and reliability with less efforts.

Automation goals can be achieved by selecting the right framework that is suitable for test automation. The cost of test automation includes both development and maintenance efforts. Selecting the suitable framework and techniques helps in maintaining the lower cost and high impact solution.

The automation framework and types of framework

In general, various structures and techniques are used to design the framework. Broadly based on these techniques and structures, we can classify the framework as follows:

- **Linear**: In this the script is created in a linear fashion, usually generated by recording and replaying without or with only slight modification.
- **Data-driven**: Parameterizes the test and fetches data from a persistent data source. The data source could be internal or external to the test.
- **Modular**: A modular framework is designed to achieve modularity at test as well as script levels. The modular framework can be of the following combinations:
  - Test script modular framework
  - Test library modular framework
- **Keyword-driven**: Keyword-driven framework is designed for reducing the maintenance cost by separating test cases from their execution.
- **Hybrid**: In this, two or more of the previous patterns are used.

Record and replay

Recording is the process of capturing an object and its properties, creating the test objects, and storing them in the Object Repository with hierarchy. Assign a logical name to the test object and create the scripts by capturing the operation performed on the GUI.

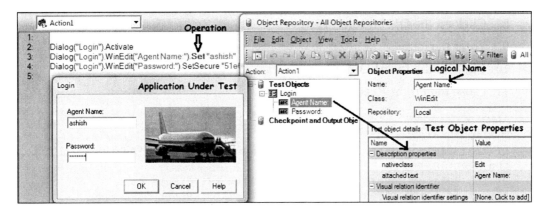

The preceding screenshot shows the AUT, recorded script, and OR. The AUT contains the test objects. OR stores the test objects in an hierarchy and with their identification properties:

The recorded scripts take us through the following three test steps:

1. Click on the **Login** dialog.
2. Enter `ashish` in the Agent Name textbox.
3. Enter the password.

A test step contains test objects with hierarchy, operation, and data value (if applicable) for the test object. While recording the user action on AUT, OR creation and scripts generation almost happen simultaneously. This approach is also called the **QTP linear framework** approach. In the linear framework approach, scripts are recorded in a step-by-step fashion without focusing on reusability. Consider an example where you have a test case to log in to an application, search for some data and then log out. In the linear framework, the code would look like something shown in the following example:

Steps for creating the QTP linear framework:

1. Enter username.
2. Enter password.

3.   Click on the **OK** button.

4.   Enter the **Flight** date.

5.   Select **Fly From** (source).

6.   Select **Fly To** (destination).

7.   Click on the **FLIGHT** button.

8.   Click on the **OK** button.

9.   Enter the name.

10. Click on the **Insert Order** button.

11. Close the **Flight Reservation** window.

```
'Login
Dialog("DialogLogin").Activate
Dialog("DialogLogin").WinEdit("EditAgentName:").Set "ashish"      'Enter
the agent name
Dialog("DialogLogin").WinEdit("EditPassword:").SetSecure
"51e6911da82a99155f73b209eaeac51a66ef0883" ' Enter password
'Create Order
Window("WinFlight").Activate
Window("WinFlight").ActiveX("MaskEdBox").Type "111114"
'Enter Flight Date
Window("WinFlight").WinComboBox("FlyFrom").Select "London"   ' Select
Source
Window("WinFlight").WinComboBox("Fly To:").Select "Frankfurt"
'Select destination
Window("WinFlight").WinButton("btnFLIGHT").Click
'Click on flight button
Window("WinFlight").Dialog("FlightTable").WinButton("btnOK").Click
'Click on the OK button
Window("WinFlight").WinEdit("EditName:").Set "Mr. James Anderson"
'Enter the passenger name
Window("WinFlight").WinButton("btnInsertOrder").Click
'Click on the Insert Order button
Window("WinFlight").Activate
Window("WinFlight").Close
'Click on the close button
```

This is the simplest way to create scripts and use and implement them if the AUT is small, but do not expect frequent changes in AUT. The normal record and playback falls under this framework.

Advantages and disadvantages of linear a framework

The advantages of linear framework are stated as follows:

- No expertize or experience of programming or designing is required. Basic knowledge of QTP is required for creating scripts.

- Automatic test object creation and storage in the Object Repository.

- This is the fastest way to create test automation scripts.

- This is the simplest framework, and it is easy to understand.

- Helps to learn the objects and create the scripts manually.

- Can add checkpoints easily.

The disadvantages of linear framework are stated as follows:

- Does not allow reusability since scripts are created in a linear fashion and do not have functions.

- Data is bound with the scripts; hence, the test is noniterative, and this approach is inefficient for executing the test for multiple sets of data. Change the data manually for each run or create multiple copies of scripts; unfortunately, both of these techniques are inefficient.

- The maintenance cost is very high, and it is tedious, and error-prone since it is required to make changes in all the affected areas.

- Need to add comments on our own.

Introduction to the data-driven framework

A data-driven framework is the collection of test scripts that run with related multiple datasets. This framework provides reusable scripts for different sets of data and it improves the test coverage. Input and result (test criteria) data values can be stored in one or more central data sources or databases; the actual format and organization can be implementation specific.

To understand the data-driven framework implementation we should know three terms:

- **Variable**
- **Parameter**
- **Iteration**

A variable is a storage location and an associated with an identifier, which contains some known or unknown quantity or information, a value.

A parameter is a variable that is provided as an input to the scripts. Parameterization in QTP can be achieved by the `datatable` object. The `datatable` object represents the QuickTest design-time data table and its associated sheets and parameters. The `datatable` object has various methods and properties to access data from the runtime data table object.

Iteration is a process where a parameterized script executes the test for a predefined number of times from a data source.

There are four major steps in creating a data-driven framework:

1. Create a script.
2. Define the parameters that hold data.
3. Add code to get data from the data source and assign a value.
4. Modify the settings or add code to execute the test for all the rows or subset of rows.

There are two major ways to access data in QTP:

- Using `datatable` object
- Using external data source

Creating data-driven scripts using the `datatable` object:

1. Create the script by recording or manually.
2. Define parameters in an external Excel sheet as shown in the following screenshot. Make sure that the first row contains the parameter name. Enter data in the subsequent rows as shown in the following screenshot:

	A	B	C	D	E	F
1	UserName	Password	Flight	FlyForm	FlyTo	Agent
2	ashish	mercury	111114	London	Paris	harsha
3	ashish	mercury	111114	London	Paris	ashish
4	ashish	mercury	111114	London	Paris	dinesh

To fetch the data from the external excel sheet, use the `import` method of `datatable`:

1. Define parameters using the `datatable` object

2. To add the data, rename the column name by double-clicking on the column name. Rename the column and add data to the subsequent rows as shown in the following screenshot:

	UserName	Password	Flight	FlyForm	FlyTo	Agent
1	ashish	mercury	111114	London	Paris	harsha
2	ashish	mercury	111114	London	Paris	ashish
3	ashish	mercury	111114	London	Paris	dinesh

3. Use the data-driver tool or `datatable` object parameterization. Add the test data to `datatable`, add the column name to the header, and double-click on **Add** or change the column name to parameter in the data table.

4. Make the test scripts iterative.

There are two ways to make scripts iterative. First, under **Test Settings** select **Run one iteration only**, **Run on all rows**, and then **Run from row** n **to row** m:

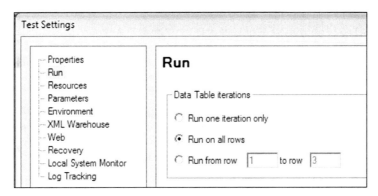

Second, you can also programmatically create the scripts for running the test script:

```
'Set the current row to retrieve the value from datatable
datatable.SetCurrentRow startnum
For i =startnum to endnum 'run the script from row (n) to row (m)
.
.
.
'Move to next row of datatable
datatable.SetNextRow
Next
```

> To run for one iteration, startnum and endnum should be 1, startnum=endnum=1
>
> To run test for all rows, startnum = 1 and endnum = datatable. datatable.GetRowCount.

Let's club all the concepts together to parameterize the test. Creating the test data in datatable. datatable takes two arguments: parameter name and sheet type. datatable has two types of sheets: local sheet (local to action) and global sheet. To access the data from the global sheet, use dtGlobalSheet, and to access the data from the local sheet, use dtLocalSheet. Refer to the following example:

```
Systemutil.Run PathToFlightApp
Dialog("DialogLogin").Activate
Dialog("DialogLogin").WinEdit("EditAgentName:").Set DataTable("Agent",
dtGlobalSheet)
Dialog("DialogLogin").WinEdit("EditPassword:").SetSecure DataTable("Pa
ssword",dtGlobalSheet)
Dialog("DialogLogin").WinButton("btnOK").Click
Window("WinFlight").ActiveX("MaskEdBox").Type DataTable("FlightDate",
dtGlobalSheet)
Window("WinFlight").WinComboBox("FlyFrom").Select DataTable("FlyFrom",
dtGlobalSheet)
Window("WinFlight").WinComboBox("Fly To:").Select DataTable("Flyto",d
tGlobalSheet)
Window("WinFlight").WinButton("btnFLIGHT").Click
Window("WinFlight").Dialog("FlightTable").WinButton("btnOK").Click
Window("WinFlight").WinEdit("EditName:").Set DataTable("Name",
dtGlobalSheet)
Window("WinFlight").WinButton("btnInsertOrder").Click
Window("WinFlight").WinButton("btnButton").Click
Window("WinFlight").Close
```

The following code shows how to import and iterate the test using datatable:

```
datatable.Import "c:\FlightData.xls"
' Import the excel to the datatable.
rc = datatable.GetRowCount
'get the row count
For i = 1 to rc
systemutil.Run PathToFlightApp
Dialog("DialogLogin").Activate
Dialog("DialogLogin").WinEdit("EditAgentName:").Set datatable.
Value("Agent")
```

```
'Value is DataTable default property. Retrieves or sets the value of
the cell in the specified parameter and the current row of the run-
time Data Table.
'To find the value use DataTable.Value(ParameterID [, SheetID])
.SheetID Optional. Identifies the sheet to be returned. The SheetID
can be the sheet name, index or dtLocalSheet, or dtGlobalSheet.
Dialog("DialogLogin").WinEdit("EditPassword:").SetSecure datatable.
Value("Password")
Dialog("DialogLogin").WinButton("btnOK").Click
Window("WinFlight").ActiveX("MaskEdBox").Type datatable.
Value("FlightDate")
Window("WinFlight").WinComboBox("FlyFrom").Select datatable.
Value("FlyFrom")
Window("WinFlight").WinComboBox("Fly To:").Select datatable.
Value("Flyto")
Window("WinFlight").WinButton("btnFLIGHT").Click
Window("WinFlight").Dialog("FlightTable").WinButton("btnOK").Click
Window("WinFlight").WinEdit("EditName:").Set datatable.Value("Name")
Window("WinFlight").WinButton("btnInsertOrder").Click
Window("WinFlight").WinButton("btnButton").Click
Window("WinFlight").Close
datatable.SetNextRow
Next
```

Using the Excel application with VBScript:

```
Set excelfile = createobject("excel.application")

'Create the excel first before executing script.
'Ensure that excel file is in Closed state.

excelfile.Workbooks.Open "D:\parameter.xls"
set sheet = excelfile.ActiveWorkbook.Worksheets("Sheet1")
  'Get the max row occupied in the excel file
Row = sheet.UsedRange.Rows.Count

'Read the data from the excel file
For i= 2 to Row

Username=sheet.cells(i,1).value
Password=sheet.cells(i,2).value
wait 1
  Next
```

```
'Close the Workbook
excelfile.ActiveWorkbook.Close

'Close Excel
excelfile.Application.Quit

'Release the objects
Set sheet =nothing
Set excelfile = nothing
```

The FileSystemObject object model

VBScript allows you to process drives, folders, and files using the FileSystemObject (FSO) object model, which is explained in the following section that describes how you can use FileSystemObject to manipulate files.

There are two ways for file manipulation:

- Creating and appending files, removing data from the files, and reading from the files
- Copying, moving, and deleting files

The following are the steps for reading and writing data from text files:

1. Create a text file.
2. Write data to it.
3. Close it.
4. Open the text file again.
5. Read the file.
6. Close it.

The following is an example of reading and writing to the text file:

```
Dim filefso, file1, readfile, s
   Const ForReading = 1
'create the object of a File system Object
   Set filefso = CreateObject("Scripting.FileSystemObject")
   Set file1 = filefso.CreateTextFile("c:\logfile.txt", True)
   'Write a line.
      file1.WriteLine "Testing FSO"
   file1.WriteBlankLines(2)
   file1.Close
```

```
   'Read contents of the text file.
   'Reading file
   Set readfile = filefso.OpenTextFile("c:\logfile.txt", ForReading)
   's = readfile.ReadLine
 'iterate the file until end of the file
Do While readfile.AtEndOfStream <> True
      retstring = readfile.ReadLine
   Loop
      ts.Close
```

An example of using a text file for data-driven testing is given as follows:

```
Dim fso, f1, textfile, s
   Const ForReading = 1

Set textfile = fso.OpenTextFile("c:\logfile.txt", ForReading)
   's = textfile.ReadLine
 'iterate the file until end of the file
Do While textfile.AtEndOfStream <> True
      retstring = textfile.ReadLine
Dialog("DialogLogin").Activate
Dialog("DialogLogin").WinEdit("EditAgentName:").Set datatable.
Value("Agent")
'Value is DataTable default property. Retrieves or sets the value of
the cell in the specified parameter and the current row of the run-
time Data Table.
'To find the value use DataTable.Value(ParameterID [, SheetID])
.SheetID Optional. Identifies the sheet to be returned. The SheetID
can be the sheet name, index or dtLocalSheet, or dtGlobalSheet.
Dialog("DialogLogin").WinEdit("EditPassword:").SetSecure datatable.
Value("Password")
Dialog("DialogLogin").WinButton("btnOK").Click
Window("WinFlight").ActiveX("MaskEdBox").Type datatable.
Value("FlightDate")
Window("WinFlight").WinComboBox("FlyFrom").Select datatable.
Value("FlyFrom")
Window("WinFlight").WinComboBox("FlyTo:").Select datatable.
Value("Flyto")
Window("WinFlight").WinButton("btnFLIGHT").Click
Window("WinFlight").Dialog("FlightTable").WinButton("btnOK").Click
Window("WinFlight").WinEdit("EditName:").Set datatable.Value("Name")
Window("WinFlight").WinButton("btnInsertOrder").Click
Window("WinFlight").WinButton("btnButton").Click
Window("WinFlight").Close

   Loop
      textfile.Close
```

The methods used for performing the read and write operation on the test files are listed as follows:

Write	Write to an opened text file
WriteLine	Write to an open text file and add a newline character to it
WriteBlankLines	Write blank line(s) to an opened text file
Read	Read characters from the text file, which are specified as an argument
ReadLine	Read the entire line, excluding the newline character
ReadAll	Read the entire data from a text file

The following example demonstrates the file manipulation operations:

```
Dim filefso, txtfile1, txtfile2, txtfifle3
    Set filefso = CreateObject("Scripting.FileSystemObject")
    Set txtfile1 = filefso.CreateTextFile("d:\tmp\testfile.txt", True)
    'Write a line.
    txtfile1.Write ("Writing a text")
    'Close the file to writing.
    txtfile1.Close
    'Moving the file to d:\tmp
    'Get a handle of the file in root of d:\.
    Set txtfile2 = filefso.GetFile("d:\tmp\testfile.txt")
    'Moving the file to tmp directory.
    txtfile2.Move ("d:\tmp\testfile.txt")

    'Copying the file to temp.
    txtfile2.Copy ("d:\temp\testfile.txt")

    Set txtfifle2 = filefso.GetFile("d:\tmp\testfile.txt")
    Set txtfifle3 = filefso.GetFile("d:\temp\testfile.txt")
    'Deleting the files
    txtfifle2.Delete
    txtfifle3.Delete
```

The following is an example of using the ADODB to get data from the database:

```
Set Conn = CreateObject("ADODB.Connection")

'Set the Connection String.
Conn.ConnectionString =
"DSN=QT_Flight32;DBQ=C:\Program Files\Mercury Interactive\QuickTest
Professional\samples\flight\app\flight32.mdb;Driver=C:\WINDOWS\
system32\odbcjt32.dll;DriverId=281;FIL=MS Access;MaxBufferSize=2048;
PageTimeout=5;"
'ADODB.Connection
'RecordSet
Conn.Open("DSN=QT_Flight32")
Set rcRecordSet= Conn.Execute("SELECT order_number from Orders order
by order_number desc")
rcRecordSet.MoveFirst
var_order_num = rcRecordSet.fields("Order_Number")
rcRecordSet.close

Conn.close
set rcRecordSet = nothing
set Conn = nothing
```

Introduction to the modular framework

Modularity allows decomposing the components and/or functionality and recombines them. This approach is a design technique that emphasizes on separating the functionality of an AUT into independent, interconnected modules such that each module contains everything necessary to execute only one aspect of the desired functionality.

Achieving the modularity requires modularity at two different layers; one layer is test and the other layer is script. To create a modular framework, we need to decompose the test layer into manageable pieces based on their objectives. For example, common test libraries are separate from function libraries. At test level, we decompose the key libraries and resources into a structure to achieve the automation goals using appropriate design.

There are four distinct parts of the modular framework:

- Script-level modularity
- Test-level modularity
- Resource structure
- Framework design

Let's take the example of the Flight application; the entire functionality can be divided into small independent functions as shown in the following figure. This requires to achieve script-level modularity as shown in the following figure:

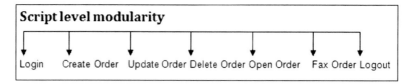

 We can omit a few functions as part of the automation that are least used and do not contribute towards ROI, such as graph, edit, and help in the Flight application.

Apart from decomposing the entire functionality into small, independent functions, we need to ensure that other components should also be decomposed. After decomposing, the entire test component look likes the following figure:

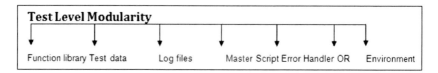

The preceding list contains the most frequently used components, but implementation of the framework may require having a few more or less components based on the automation goals and requirements. Following is the description of these components:

- **Function library**: This is a collection of scripts that perform a particular task. Usually one task that allows to perform on the set of statements on AUT.
- **Test data**: This is stored in `datatable`, or an external data source provides the input for the tests.
- **Log files**: They capture the log message that is used to see the outcome of the test scripts.

- **Master scripts**: These drive the flow of the test and allow coordination with the other components to ensure that the test runs successfully.

- **Error handlers**: These allow to exit the test gracefully when an error occurs, and reveal information about the error.

- **OR**: This is a part of the test that contains the test object; usually the OR is a shared OR.

- **Environment**: This is a component used to provide test-level environment variables or values that allow configuration of the tests that have to be run on various environments.

Structure

After the test is decomposed, resources are required to be arranged in a structured way, which means there is a centralized repository for these resources. Managing the test requires the folder structure or test management tool (for example, Quality Center) to store the test resources. We need to ensure that the test component stays as defined by the guidelines and structure. Structure allows organizing the resources for achieving portability and consistency. The framework's folder structure is as shown in the following screenshot. The structure may vary from project to project but it's important for achieving consistency.

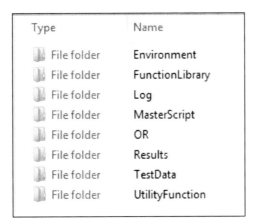

Type	Name
File folder	Environment
File folder	FunctionLibrary
File folder	Log
File folder	MasterScript
File folder	OR
File folder	Results
File folder	TestData
File folder	UtilityFunction

Advantages

Structure has the following advantages:

- **Facilitates specialization**: Structure designs the components to perform the specific tasks and provide abstraction from complexity.

- **Control over resources**: Resource structure simplifies control over resources because they are at centralized locations and governed by policies for accessing, creating, and updating the resources.

- **Easier communication**: Resource structures clearly state the flow of information in a controlled way among team members. The modifications are done at a centralized location and utilized by all the other team members.

- **Better performance**: Each component is specialized to perform its task and is tested thoroughly to improve the performance and reliability of the test.

 Always use the relative path; do not hardcode the resource location in scripts.

Design

Design is the most important aspect of frameworks. The design of a framework is driven by its key automation goals. The following is a comprehensive but not complete list of goals, where a few more goals can be added if required:

- **Maintainability**: It allows decomposing of resources and scripts; this make it easier to maintain and debug, and to fix the issues faster and reliably.

- **Readability**: It is a well-designed and smaller function that improves the readability of the script and makes it easy to understand as well as enhances it.

 Comments and script/function headers are important to improve the readability and understandability.

- **Extensibility**: When small functions are created and resources are structured, extending the existing functionality becomes easy. This allows us to add and enhance functionality, debug, and test with ease faster.

- **Reusability**: Functions that allow reusability to function make the framework robust and reliable.

 Before we start designing the framework, we should think of functions that can be used across scripts in the test to increase the reusability. Test these common functions thoroughly, and make sure that they have the necessary error handling capabilities.

- **Concise scripts**: Make sure that scripts are short and do a single task at a time; these scripts should be a part of the appropriate libraries or modules. Ensure that the scripts are tightly cohesive and loosely coupled.

High cohesion and coupling

Coupling refers to that part of the code which can be reused and can be separated from the code but is part of it directly. Whereas cohesion is a measure of how closely related are all the responsibilities, data, and methods of a class/code to each other.

In particular, I would like to achieve a minimum of three specific things with the design and architecture of a framework:

- Keep things that have to change together in the code, as close together as possible.
- Allow unrelated things in the code to change independently (also known as orthogonality).

  Orthogonality is a concept that allows combining the small components to get effective results. This eases the read/write programs. A more orthogonal design allows for fewer exceptions, symmetry, and consistency.

- Minimize duplication in the code.

The goals behind achieving loose coupling between modules are:

- Make the code easier to read
- Make our codes easier to consume by other developers by hiding the complexity
- Isolate potential changes to a small area of code
- Reuse code in completely new contexts

Decreasing coupling and increasing cohesion

We generally consider high cohesion to be a good thing for designing framework libraries like a key design considerations, but why?

Look at the following code. We need a connection string to connect to the database, and the connection string and database manipulation code is tightly coupled. Alright, what is the issue here? Now if we want to change the DSN, we need to change the code for each DSN:

```
Set Conn = CreateObject("ADODB.Connection")
Conn.Open("DSN=QT_Flight32")
Set rcRecordSet= Conn.Execute("SELECT order_number from Orders
  order by order_number desc")
rcRecordSet.MoveFirst
var_order_num = rcRecordSet.fields("Order_Number")
rcRecordSet.close


Conn.close
set rcRecordSet = nothing
set Conn = nothing
```

Let's rewrite this code to make it less coupled and highly cohesive. I have divided the code into two parts. The first part is a function that returns the DSN, and the second part uses that DSN and manipulates the database. Now if the user wants to access another database, the DSN will be different and the user just needs to change the parameter. The previous code is coupled and the following code is cohesive:

```
Function getDSN(database)
If database = "access"
 DSN ="DSN=QT_Flight32"
ELSEIF
...
End Function

Set Conn = CreateObject("ADODB.Connection")
Conn.Open(getDSN("access") )
Set rcRecordSet= Conn.Execute("SELECT order_number from Orders
  order by order_number desc")
rcRecordSet.MoveFirst
var_order_num = rcRecordSet.fields("Order_Number")
rcRecordSet.close
Conn.close
set rcRecordSet = nothing
set Conn = nothing
```

There is one more design consideration in the context of the QTP, that is, whether we should use actions or functions.

From my personal experience, we should use functions. Actions have many advantages and should be preferred in implementing any framework. Functions allow us to achieve the goals without functional decomposition. To create the framework, the generic library is required; for example, Logger, Error handler, and configuration utilities are required to achieve the following:

The usability can be enhanced by dividing the entire flow into small manageable pieces using actions or functions.

Key steps for designing the modular framework are as follows:

- Analyze the application
- Create the design
- Create Automation Test Repository
- Create the test-level components
- Create the script-level functions
- Integrate
- Test It

Analyzing the application

Analyzing the application defines the automation goals into the defined functions and operations of the intended application. The key considerations for the analysis are:

- What are the key functionalities of the application and how are they related to each other?
- What are key flows?
- Which is the least used functionality? Will it contribute to ROI?
- What are the goals that we want to achieve through automation?

Creating a design

Creating a design describes the desired features and operations in detail, including layouts, modules, rules, verification, and interaction among modules along with the process diagrams, pseudo code, and other documentation.

The key to achieving modularity is by decomposing the functionality and recombining the modules:

- **Decomposition**: The interaction of the user with the application is broken down into libraries, such as Functional library (login, createorder, and so on), Common library, OR, Test data, and environment.

- **Recombination**: The basic elements of interaction are recombined to follow a formal test plan using several levels of aggregation. The steps are aggregated to make sequences of the basic steps, and the sequences of basic steps are combined to make a scenario. The scenarios are aggregated to make a test suite.

After decomposition and recombination, the overall modular framework design will look like the following diagram:

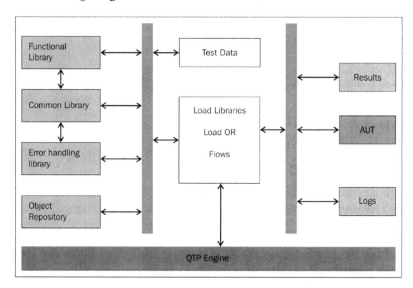

Setting up an environment

Perform the following steps to set up the test environment:

1. Create the structure, which is the same as creating the infrastructure for the test.

2. Create resources, including installation.

3. Create the folder structures or resources in the Test Management tool.

4. Ensure version control (good practice).

5. Create the configuration file.

Creating Object Repository

Create the OR by adding objects (Add objects to local repository or record the test step that automatically creates the test objects).

Creating test-level components

Perform the following steps to create test-level components:

1. Prepare the test data.
2. Create common functions/libraries.
3. Create a functional library.
4. Create test flows.
5. Add common components by loading the libraries.

Creating script-level functions

Perform the following steps to create script-level components:

1. Create steps manually.
2. Add the required programming logic.
3. Call the common functions (verification points).
4. Call the `err` handlers.

Integrating design elements

Bring all the pieces together into a testing environment, and ensure that the test automation is working end-to-end.

Test the framework design

Finally, we can perform the test to checks for errors, bugs, and interoperability.

Report the bugs, fix them, and retest.

Advantages of modular frameworks

- Functional decomposition allows us to divide and conquer the complexities
- Modularity eases designing, implementing, and debugging of the frameworks
- Provides standard interfaces for communicating with each other and allows the plugging in and removal of the new modules

Challenges for modular frameworks

The key challenges for creating modular frameworks are as follows:

- Require more technical know-how and effort to create generic modules
- For very specific modules, the cost of making interfaces is high
- For assemblers (integrators), it can be difficult to assess the quality and interaction of different modules
- It can be difficult to assemble (integrate) the modules
- The design creativity of a module designer can be limited because he needs to conform to the interface
- Less variation in products because of overuse of the same modules
- Total system performance may be suboptimal

The keyword-driven framework

Keyword-driven testing is also called table-driven testing or action-based testing. It is a software testing methodology.

Keyword-driven testing uses a spreadsheet to specify test cases in a specific format, usually in a table format. The functions are designed for each keyword. This keyword is stored in the column on a row of the table. For example, in the keyword-driven approach, each action has its corresponding function stored in the functional library. Driver scripts drive the entire flow, fetch the action, and call the corresponding function.

The keyword-driven testing approach

The keyword-driven approach is when the interaction of a user with an application is abstracted in the form of actions, and data is maintained in the external source.

Decomposition

The interaction of the user with the application is broken down to the basic elements (login, select flight ...). In the keyword-driven approach, a keyword represents the business scenario that performs many actions on AUT or small actions repeatedly. The basic elements of interaction are referred to as steps.

Recombination

The basic elements of interaction are recombined to follow a formal test plan using several levels of aggregation. The steps are aggregated to make sequence(s) of the basic steps, and sequences of the basic steps are combined to make sequence groups.

Refer to the following screenshot that shows mapping of the actions from its library function using driver script. The interaction of a user with an application is abstracted in the form of actions and data maintained in the external source.

Separate the test cases from the scripts. The test cases are kept out of the scripts. These are fetched by the driver script and the `keyword` function is called as shown in the following screenshot:

Action	MR	Data
Login	No	UserName=ashish;Password=mercury
CloseDialog	No	NA
SelectFlightsOptions	No	Pessenger=2;Trip=oneway; from=Frankfurt;to=London;TravelClass=First;Prefrence=Blue Skies Airlines
SelectFlight	No	NA
VerBookingData	No	NA
SetNamenMeals	Yes	FirstName0=Ashish;LastName0=bhargava;meal=Hindu,FirstName1=Neeti;LastName1=sharma;meal=Hindu
SetCreditCardDetails	No	creditCard=American Express;cc_num=1234567890;exp_mn=12;exp_year=2010;firstname=Ian;midname=K;lastname=sharma
SetBillingAddress	No	address1=address1;address2=address2;city=newyork;statenewyork;zip=11111;country=UNITED STATES
SetDeliveryAddress	No	address1=address1;address2=address2;city=newyork;statenewyork;zip=11111;country=UNITED STATES
SetTicketLess	No	Yes
SetCopyAddress	No	NA
BookFlight	No	NA
GetConfirmationNumber	No	NA
GetTotalTaxnPrice	No	NA
Home	No	NA

```
Select Case ( Action)
Case "Login"

If ( trim(Data) <> "NA" ) Then
ActLogin  Data
else
ActLogin
End IF
```

Once the keyword is found, the corresponding keyword library function is called as shown in the following screenshot:

```
1    Public Function ActLogin (ldata)
2        'Author
3        'Description
4        'Create Date
5        SyncPage "LoginPage","LoginPage"
6
7        userdata = Split(ldata,";")
8        name = Mid(userdata(0), InStr(userdata(0),"=") + 1 )
9        'msgbox name
10       password =Mid(userdata(1), Instr(userdata(1),"=") + 1 )
11
12       'msgbox password
13
14
15       Browser("LoginPage").Page("LoginPage").WebEdit("userName").Set name
16       Browser("LoginPage").Page("LoginPage").WebEdit("password").Set password
17       Browser("LoginPage").Page("LoginPage").Image("Sign-In").Click
18
19       Reporter.ReportEvent micPass ,"Login", "Pass"
20       WriteToLog logfilepath, "Pass","Login","username ashish and password mercury"
21
22   End Function
23
```

Development of the keyword-driven framework requires achieving the modularity first; apart from that, we need the keyword function library, test cases, and driver script. The keyword-driven framework is a modular framework plus test cases stored in an external source and driver scripts with a specific functional library, also called the keyword library.

Function decomposition is an important activity for designing the keyword-driven framework, and the decomposition guide to identify the keywords. Keywords are the reusable functions that perform one of the key action(s) on AUT, do a specific task, and complete it on their own terms. Another important aspect of the keyword-driven framework is test cases are separated from the test scripts.

The keyword-driven or test-plan driven method

This approach leverages the advantages of functional decomposition and separates the execution from the scripts. The test cases are defined in the spreadsheet containing the keywords. Each keyword has its corresponding function library that performs the action on the AUT.

In this method, the entire process is keyword driven, including the functionality. The keywords control the processing.

Keyword-driven testing (KDT) was created to simplify the creation of automated test cases and make them as much as manual test cases. KDT creates QTP-automated test scripts On the Fly based on information entered into a spreadsheet.

Test case representation will be in rows and columns. In the test scenario spreadsheet, each test case will perform an action.

 In automated testing, the lowest level of granularity is the test case step. The step level is where each action or verification occurs.

As per KDT, we need to prepare data spreadsheets for each locale because the functionality may differ based upon the different locales. Some locales have a specific coverage for commercial groups, individual businesses, and so on. It is difficult to handle these in the test script. Test suite is prepared to specify which locale/locales need to be executed, and the script is made generic. The script is driven based on the Excel sheet, which will take Excel data from the locale and generate the On the Fly script.

Key steps for designing the keyword-driven framework:

1. Analyze the application.
2. Create the design.
3. Create the Automation Test Repository.
4. Create the test-level components.
5. Create the scripts-level functions.
6. Integrate.
7. Test it.

We have already seen the key steps in creating the modular framework. The approach remains the same for the keyword-driven framework as well.

Let's find out about the automation repository in the keyword-driven approach. Overall, it contains data related to documents, test suite, and created test cases and libraries.

Test cases are also referred to as test scenarios or test groups, which contain the spreadsheet that specifies the test steps for execution.

Common libraries contain the QTP library files and (.vbs, .qfl) files that control the entire KDT control flow, for example, driver scripts and library files (.qfl, .vbs). Common libraries can be viewed as:

- Utility functions
- Navigation functions
- Support functions

Environment libraries contain .xml and .qfl files that are used to set the environment.

Error libraries contain files that are used to catch the errors during execution and perform the necessary actions (.qfl or .vbs file).

Framework documents contain all the data that is created for the framework, for example, enhancements to the initial framework or help files created for the framework.

Object Repository contains the .tsr object files created using QTP.

The following diagram shows how various layers and components work together to achieve the overall design:

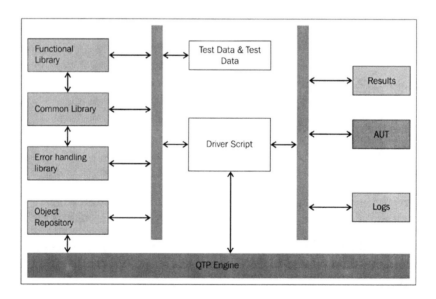

Generic flow in keyword-driven approach

The key steps and their sequence of execution in the keyword-driven approach are as follows:

1. Fetch the keyword as mentioned in the spreadsheet.
2. Build a list of the parameters from the step that follows.
3. Call the utility functions; the utility scripts will do the following:
    1. Call utility scripts with the input parameter-list received from the utility script.
    2. Call the driver script to perform specific tasks (for example, log in, select flight, and so on), calling user-defined functions if required.
    3. Report any errors to a test report for the test case.
    4. Exception handler scripts.
    5. Return to the driver script.
4. Repeat the steps from 1 to 3.

Advantages of the keyword-driven approach

The key advantages offered by the keyword-driven approach are as explained in the following sections.

Cost effectiveness

The keyword-driven automation framework reduces cost and time of the test design, automation, and execution. Keywords are highly reusable functions that represent the business scenarios or actions performed on the GUI. Each of these well-designed and tested functions provide good return on investment over a period of time.

Separating test cases allows executing test cases without modifying the scripts. When the flow of the application changes, just change the test cases and not the scripts.

Reusability

Keywords, utilities, and functions are built to achieve reusability. The entire framework is divided into layers that are integrated with each other.

Ease of maintenance

- The keyword-driven approach provides abstraction from the complexities and technical challenges; it is easy to maintain

- The robustness of the keyword-driven framework allows adapting the changes in GUI and test flows

- Allows focusing on the development of test cases without or with minimal changes to the scripts, functions, and utilities

Ease of execution

The keyword-driven approach allows executing and creating automated test cases for non-technical testers, business analysts, and SMEs (Subject Matter Expert) to write automated tests.

Test cases are separated from the scripts, and it is easy to prepare the test cases using the used keywords without knowledge of how they have been implemented.

Key challenges

Knowledge of designing is required.

New team members have to put in efforts to understand the framework and its design. Good documentation and knowledge sharing is required to overcome this issue.

The hybrid framework

The **hybrid framework** allows combining the two frameworks to leverage their strengths and remove their weaknesses. Most frameworks, which are developed, fall into this category that uses the function decomposition like modular frameworks and the data-driven approach.

Key steps in designing the hybrid framework are as follows:

1. Creating the folder structure.
2. Creating and storing automation resources.
3. Organizing and managing resources.
4. Integrating the frameworks.
5. Dry run.

Advantages of the hybrid framework

Hybrid framework allows leverages, and pulls the strengths of the other frameworks and eliminates their shortcomings, which suits the automation. Practically, most of the test automation solutions fall in this category.

Key challenges

Though it mitigates the weaknesses of the other approaches, it loses its generosity and is very specific to the test automation solution AUT, which reduces the reusability of its components across the multiple AUTs.

Business Process Testing

Business Process Testing (BPT) approach allows dividing the business processes into smaller reusable components that can used many times in the same or different test scripts; for example, the business process of buying a product is split into components such as log in, select product, add to cart, place order, and log out, which can be re-used in the same business process or different processes. The key advantage is it facilitates SMEs, Bas, and automation engineers to work and collaborate effectively. Some people call it a framework, but this is an approach rather than a framework. BPT is similar to the modular approach of creating test automation solutions using QTP and Quality Center.

Application-independent framework

The application-independent framework is a specific keyword-driven testing or table-driven testing. It identifies the keywords that are independent of the AUT, which can perform specific actions on the components of the AUT directly. The key difference between the keyword-driven framework and application-independent keyword-driven framework lies in the library. In the application-independent keyword-driven framework, the functional library is more generic or works directly on the generic components for AUT. The following is the data table:

Window	WinObject	Action	Arguments
Calculator	button	Click	1
Calculator	button	Click	+
Calculator	button	Click	3
Calculator	button	Click	=
Calculator	Text	VerResult	4

The functionality of the AUT is specified in the data table. The preceding table allows calculating some operations on the calculator window, which is 1 + 3 = and verify the result. The instructions are as follows:

1. Click on the button (**1**) in the calculator window.
2. Click on the button (**+**) in the calculator window.
3. Click on the button (**3**) in the calculator window.
4. Click on the button (**=**) in the calculator window.
5. Verify the result from text in the calculator.

The action column lists the actions done with the mouse, keyboard, or specific functions. The data table should be mapped to generate the test step; for example, mouse click on the button, and the button is identified by the argument (1). The control name is given in the `WinObject` column, and the `Window` column contains the name of the application.

In QTP, the Object Repository stores the test objects and provides the logical name | to it. We can use this logical name as a parameter to create the script; for example, we can store the object hierarchy in Excel with data. That is, utilizing the code to create the application-independent frameworks. The following diagram is an example of how we can achieve the application-independent implementation using excel and convert it into scripts. All the objects' names are provided in the column; in runtime, it fetches the object information and creates the scripts as shown in the following diagram:

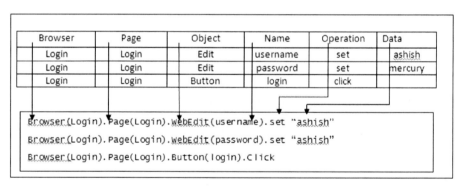

In the preceding diagram, we can observe that the script creates the objects at runtime rather than the hardcoded scripts. This gives the application independence from the other applications.

Advantages of the application-independent framework

Application-independent keyword-driven framework inherits all the advantages of the keyword-driven framework, apart from the one that allows us to work on different applications without much changes.

Key challenges of the application-independent framework

Creating the application-independent framework requires more expertise to deal with the complexities in creating generic libraries.

The application-independent keyword-driven approach is usually designed for specific technologies and not for multiple technologies.

The most basic framework that is provided by QTP is the replay mechanism and easy steps to create the test steps. These steps are put into reusable functions and become the functional library in the modular and keyword-driven frameworks. Parameterizing the step and allowing it to iterate becomes the data-driven approach. Refer to the following diagram that shows the steps we performed in developing the one framework that became the base for developing the next one, for example, record and replay become the base for data-driven frameworks. One framework becomes the base or partial base to the next framework. Refer to the following diagram demonstrating how they are related:

Framework Type	Keyword	Modular	Data Driven	Record &Replay
Key Steps	Create Driver Scripts Create Test Structure Create Utility Functions Split scripts into keyword library Recording or Manual Creates scripts Replay the scripts	Create master scripts Recombine all modular components Create Utility Functions Create Test Structure Split script into functional library Recording or Manual Creates Replay the scripts	Parameterize the test and iterate it Recording or Manual Creates scripts Replay the scripts	Record script Replay script
Key Components	Keyword Library Function library Utility Functions Driver scripts Test Structure	Master Scripts Function Library Utility Functions Test Structure	Scripts Data Source	Linear Scripts QTP Engine

Summary

This chapter describes the various concepts and approaches to build a framework and its components, and a structure that allows us to keep the resources uniformly accessible. This helps to achieve the automation goals and lower the maintenance cost of the test automation suite.

In the next chapter, we are going to discuss various ways to debug scripts, custom logging deployment, and maintaining the framework.

5
Deploying and Maintaining Frameworks

In the previous chapter we learned how to design and create a test framework. The key considerations while deploying the framework are portability and configuration for the underlying environment. Debugging is an important pre deployment activity. In this chapter we will discuss the following:

- Script debugging techniques in QTP
- Pre deployment review checklist
- Customizing logs and filtering log messages
- Deploying the framework
- Maintaining the frameworks

Predeployment

Once the testing of the framework is complete and the bugs have been raised, we will start with debugging. This process tries to find what went wrong in the framework by looking at the following:

- How it failed
- Where it failed
- How to fix the bugs

Plan the debugging from the design phase and implement it by developing custom and error logs. Provide the mechanism to filter, enable, and disable the logs and features. This helps to debug the scripts both in the development and maintenance phases of framework designing. QTP provides various options for debugging scripts, actions, and functional libraries.

Debugging with QTP

QTP provides various ways to debug scripts that are a part of functional libraries or actions. To debug the script, execute it from the start to a certain step in the script or from a certain step to the end of the script or action. The following section describes the various techniques provided by QTP to debug the script. Ensure that the application is open at the relevant location before starting to debug the scripts.

Run to step

When this option is clicked on, it runs the test from the beginning of the script or action (**Expert View** only) to the current location in the test or action, and stops the execution at a particular step. To run the test from the beginning, navigate to **Resources | Run to Step** or press *Ctrl + F10*.

Debug from step

To debug from a step, instead of the beginning of the script or action, use the **Debug from Step** option; it allows you to debug from a specific step in the test or action. To debug from a specific step, navigate to **Resources | Debug from Step**.

Run from step

Instruct QTP to run the action from a particular step instead of from the beginning of the script or action. To do this, navigate to **Resources | Run from Step**.

In the **Expert View**, the **Run from Step** option runs the test from the selected script to the end of the action (or until it reaches a breakpoint). Using the **Run from Step** option in this mode ignores any iteration. However, if the action contains nested actions, QTP runs the nested actions for the defined number of iterations of the nested action.

Run from action

This option runs the test from the beginning of the script to the beginning of the selected action and then pauses the run session. Navigate to the **Test Flow** pane and right-click on **Run from Action**.

Debug from action

Instruct QTP to begin a debug session and pause it at the beginning of the selected action. Navigate to the **Test Flow** pane and right-click on **Debug from Action**.

Run to action

Instruct QTP to start a run session from the beginning of the selected action. Navigate to the **Test Flow** pane and right-click on **Run to Action**.

Debugging a functional library

Creating a framework requires creating separate function libraries. For better maintenance, the steps to debug the functional library are as follows:

1. Associate the function library with a test.

2. In your test, insert a call to at least one of the functions defined in the function library.

3. Run the test, suspend the run session, and debug the function library.

> During a debug session, all documents are read-only and cannot be edited. To edit a document during a debug session, we have to stop the debug session.
>
> The execution marker may not be displayed correctly when the test script uses the `ExecuteFile` statement.

Reviewing the checklist for predeployment

Before deployment, ensure that we review the following points (that exist in scripts or are taken care of) for lower maintenance cost of the framework:

- The test should always have a known start point.

- It should always end with the same start point.

  The test should start from a specific point and ensure that the entire infrastructure is ready for execution. It would be ideal if we create the script to check the resources that are placed for test execution. For example, if the script starts its execution by starting the AUT and closes the application at the end of execution, the next iteration or test will start from the start point for opening an application.

- The test should clean up the resources: for example, closing MS Excel, closing files, closing tests, and so on.

- Configure the values instead of hardcoding; use the environment variables as shown in the code snippet that follows, or use dictionary objects:

```
<Environment>
  <Variable>
    <Name>AppPath</Name>
    <Value>C:\Program Files\HP\QuickTest Professional\samples\
flight\app\flight4a.exe</Value>
  </Variable>
  <Variable>
    <Name>ErrFileExtn</Name>
    <Value>.bmp</Value>
  </Variable>

</Environment>
```

- Appropriate comments and script header

  The header allows us to read a brief description about the function or script as shown. This helps to make scripts and functions readable and maintainable:

```
'****************************************************
'Author
'Description
'Date Creation
'Parameters     in     out
'Change History
'Changed By Date Description
'****************************************************
```

- Readability and appropriate documentation.

- Script should be maintainable and easy to modify

  The script and function header improve readability and allow modification of the code with ease, since it reveals key information and reduces maintenance time.

- Error handling and snapshot for errors

  Ensure that the script contains the code to capture the snapshot using custom libraries, the `CaptureBitmap` method, or the `CaptureBitmap` of desktop utility.

- The test should reveal maximum information in case an error occurs.

  The error messages should be clear and concise.

- Logging utilities

  The logging utilities are a must to provide information and error logs.

- Code should have proper synchronization

  Ensure that the code has the ability to deal with synchronization issues by using `wait`, `wait` property, `exist`, `enable`, and `sync`.

- Graceful exit

  Ensure that the code appropriately allows graceful exit using `Exit Function`, `Exit For`, `Exit Test`, and `Exit Action`.

Custom logs

All of the given techniques are useful to test the scripts but when we design the framework, there must be some abstraction and a set of layers to reach the actual point of error. The custom logs reveal information about how and where the error condition has occurred. A good logging mechanism displays the relevant message and snapshots of the error as well. Custom logs should provide the following:

- Enabling logging
- Disabling logging
- Filtering logs

Enabling logging

The simplest way to debug is to use the `print` or `MsgBox` statements. The `Print` statement displays the message in the QTP log window and `MsgBox` displays the message box where the user needs to click on **OK** explicitly. It is not usually appreciable to use the `MsgBox` option since it requires human intervention, but it helps to fix the issues quickly in a few cases.

The debug version of the framework allows us to print or display messages to reveal the information required to find issues. QTP also provides the `Reporter` object to report the messages into the **Run Result** window. Apart from the `print` and `MsgBox` statements, logging is an important tool for debugging. The example that follows demonstrates how to enable or disable logging:

- Use the `Filter` property of the `Reporter` object with the `rfEnableAll` option to display all the messages using the `Reporter` object
- Use the `Debug` variable in the environment to turn the log messages `ON`
- Use the `MsgBox` statement to display the message in the window

- Use the `print` statement to print the values in QTP's print log

```
Public Function ActLogin (ldata)
    'Author
    'Description
    'Create Date
    'Set the environment variable as rfEnableAll or 0
     Reporter.Filter = Environment("DebugOption") '
    SyncPage "LoginPage","LoginPage"
    userdata = Split(ldata,";")
    name = Mid(userdata(0), InStr(userdata(0),"=") + 1 )
   print name
    password =Mid(userdata(1), Instr(userdata(1),"=") + 1 )
   print password
    Browser("LoginPage").Page("LoginPage").WebEdit("userName").Set
name
    Browser("LoginPage").Page("LoginPage").WebEdit("password").Set
password
    Browser("LoginPage").Page("LoginPage").Image("Sign-In").Click
   If Environment("Debug")  = ON
    Reporter.ReportEvent micPass ,"Login", "Pass"
    WriteToLog logfilepath, "Pass","Login","username "& username  &
and password"& password
Else
End Function
```

Disabling logs

Disabling the log messages does just the opposite of enabling the messages:

- Use the `Filter` property of the `Reporter` object with the `rfDisableAll` option to display all the messages
- Use the `Debug` variable in the environment to turn the log messages `OFF`
- Comment using the `MsgBox` statement
- Comment using the `print` statement

Filtering logs

The log message displays one of the following statuses when a test step has been executed:

- Error
- Warning

- Fail
- Done or Info

In some cases, Fatal is also a category for the log message type.

QTP's `Reporter` object allows us to display four types of messages using the `ReportEvent` method. The syntax for `ReportEvent` is shown as follows:

Reporter.ReportEvent EventStatus, ReportStepName, Details [, ImageFilePath]

The `ReportEvent` method reports an event to the **Run Result** window. This method allows us to notify the user for various events.

The following is the status of the **Run Result** window:

Event status	Action
0 or micPass	This reports the passed message to the **Run Result** window
1 or micFail	This reports the failed message to the **Run Result** window
2 or micDone	This reports the completion of the step in the **Run Result** window
3 or micWarning	This sends a warning message to the **Run Result** window

The following is an example of using the `ReportEvent` method:

```
Reporter.ReportEvent micDone, "Test Step1", "Step Done..."
Reporter.ReportEvent micPass,"Test Step3", "Step Pass"
Reporter.ReportEvent micWarning, "Test Step4", "Step Warning"
Reporter.ReportEvent micFail,"Test Step2", "Step Fail"
```

Once the `ReportEvent` method is executed, the result is shown in the **Run Result** window. The following screenshot shows the icon along with the message to indicate the possible results:

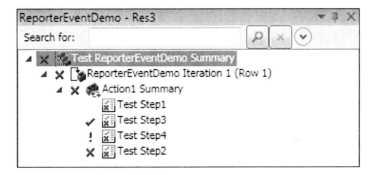

The following table lists the `Filter` options in the `Reporter` object:

EventStatus	Action
0 or `rfEnableAll`	Reports all the events to the **Run Result** window
1 or `rfEnableErrorsAndWarnings`	Reports the warning and failed status to the **Run Result** window
2 or `rfEnableErrorsOnly`	Reports the failed status to the **Run Result** window
3 or `rfDisableAll`	Does not report any status to the **Run Result** window

The test version versus the debug version

In the framework test automation, we write the debug support code (debug code) that will not be released in the final program. The debug code makes sure that the code is correct at a certain point, or that it has correct values. The debug code can also be commented and uncommented on as well. This may be time consuming, therefore we prefer ON/OFF debugging. The debug code is not executed in the test version, but in case we need to debug the code we can enable the debug code. This becomes the debug version. The following sample code shows how we can enable and disable logging:

```
Function WritetoLog ( Err_number, Err_description, custom_message)
If environment("Debug") = ON then
    Const ForReading=1 , ForAppending=8, ForWriting =2
    Dim FilesysObj, logfile,logfilepath
    logfilepath = Environment("LogFile")

    Set FilesysObj = CreateObject("Scripting.FileSystemObject")
    Set logfile = FilesysObj.OpenTextFile(logfilepath &"\log.
txt",ForAppending , true)
    logfile.WriteLine(now() &"    " &Err_number & "     "& Err_
description& "   "& custom_message)
    logfile.close()
else
endif
End Function
```

Deployment

After the test automation framework is completed and tested, it needs to be released for automation engineers, SMEs, or even business users. The release activity follows from the completed development process. It includes all the operations to prepare a system for assembly and transfer it for use. Therefore, it must determine the resources required to operate and collect information for carrying out subsequent activities of the deployment process. Deployment is a process that starts after release. In the release process, the following artifacts are delivered but may vary based on the project's need:

- Release notes
- Mapping document (traceability matrix)
- Design/architecture document
- Configuration files
- Deployment guide
- User guide

Deployment is a set of activities that makes scripts (frameworks) available for use. During the process of deployment, make sure that the QTP-required patches and add-ins are installed. Ensure that all the required parameters are configured. After deployment, the test automation repository is created in the local drive's folder or in the test management tool.

Maintenance

Maintenance includes error corrections, enhancement of capabilities, deletion of obsolete capabilities, and optimization. It is a process of evaluating, controlling, and making modifications that lead to changes in the code, GUI and flows of the application, and automation scripts. In a typical software project life cycle, maintenance leads to enhancement. A common perception of maintenance is that it merely involves fixing defects. All maintenance activities can be categorized into four classes as follows:

- **Adaptive**: This modifies the system to cope with changes in the environment or AUT.
- **Perfective**: This implements new or changed user requirements, which concern functional enhancements.
- **Corrective**: This involves diagnosing and fixing errors, possibly the ones found by users.

- **Preventive**: This increases software maintainability or reliability to prevent problems in the future.

One or more of the following are kept up-to-date as the AUT is updated over time:

- **Test objects:** When a new version or patch is released it may be required to change test objects, their properties, and adding or removing the test objects.
- **Parameters in OR:** It may be required to change the OR parameters that reflect the changes in the AUT. Update the object descriptions as the object properties may change; this can be done in the following two ways:
    - ° Manually change the object properties
    - ° Run the test in the **Update Run** mode or **Maintenance Run** mode

Both of these modes are explained in the following section.

We can delete, change, or add new releases of the test object; this results in the removal or addition of test objects. The test objects are added or removed and redistributed to the OR with changes.

Script/library maintenance

With changes in the flow, the addition of functionality and modification in the scripts and libraries needs to be updated. While designing the framework, consider how the scripts and functional libraries should be changed. In the design phase, make sure that the design is robust enough to accommodate minimal changes or no changes at all.

Automation test repository maintenance

To maintain the frameworks, we need to periodically clean up the obsolete resources or documents, such as log files, result folders, and test data.

QTP provides two options for maintaining scripts. These are explained in the following section.

The Maintenance Run mode

When the script runs in the **Maintenance Run** mode and the object has changed, it offers to update the properties and steps or keep the original object and step intact. If QTP fails to recognize the test object, it asks the user to point the object in the AUT and then provide the option to update the properties or keep the original object or step. If the changed checkpoint values are not updated, they will fail in the case of a mismatch.

The Update Run mode

The **Update Run** mode allows us to do the following:

* Update the test object descriptions
* Update the checkpoints and output values
* Update the active screen images and values

Decide on what is required to update and select the option(s) as shown in the preceding list. In the case that QTP fails to recognize the object, it will throw an error. It updates the object if the object has changed without intimating the user.

Enhancement

Enhancement starts with the analysis and assessment of the impact of changes on the scripts. Enhance the test, debug it, and then release it.

The key steps in the enhancement process are shown as follows:

* Understand the changes and their impact
* Change the scripts and document them
* Test
* Debug and fix errors
* Release

The overall goal is to achieve low maintenance cost. The issues in the maintenance phase are both managerial and technical. Test automation faces various managerial issues such as estimating costs, changing customer priorities, and staffing, whereas examples of technical issues are working with limited understanding, impact analysis, and testing. The framework allows low maintenance costs due to its test automation repository structure and standard ways to add, remove, and modify the scripts and libraries.

Summary

This chapter places emphasis on the techniques required in maintaining the framework. Debugging is an important technique for identifying and fixing the issue quickly. The next chapter talks about using JavaScript, which allows interaction with the DOM in the web page and uses XPath to create the script.

6

DOM- and XPath-based Framework in Web Applications

For web application automation, QTP allows us to use the **Document Object Model** (**DOM**) and execute JavaScript. QTP also finds the elements using **XPath**. In this chapter, we are going to learn about DOM, basic JavaScript, and XPath terminology. We'll also learn, with an example, how to use XPath to find the elements and use them in creating scripts. QTP allows executing the JavaScript code in scripts. JavaScript can use the HTML DOM for finding elements, changing HTML content, attributes, style, and removing the HTML elements.

Document Object Model

The Document Object Model (DOM) allows representation of an HTML document as a tree structure as well as allows dynamic access and updating of content, structure, and style of an HTML document.

HTML DOM

HTML DOM defines objects and properties of HTML elements and methods to access them. In simpler words, HTML DOM allows standard ways to add, retrieve, change, or delete HTML elements. In the HTML DOM everything is considered as a node:

- The entire document is a node called node document
- Each HTML element is an element node
- Text inside element is a text node

- Every attribute in a node is an attribute node
- Comment is a comment node

Node relationships – parents, children, and siblings

HTML is a mark-up language which defines tags; these tags are associated with each other in a relationship which is shown as following:

- Each document has one root element and that does not parent.
- A node can have many children but only one parent.
- Nodes sharing the same parents are called siblings.

Look at the following HTML code fragment to understand the relationship:

```
<html>
  <head>
    <title> DOM Example </title>
  </head>
  <body>
    <h1>Chapter 1</h1>
    <p>QTP</p>
  </body>
</html>
```

The relationship among the tags in the preceding script is shown as follows:

- The <html> tag is the root node and it has no parent node
- The <html> node is the parent node of the <head> and <body> tags, or in other words, the <html> node has two child nodes: <head> and <body>
- The parent node of the QTP text node is the <h1> node
- The <head> node has one child node: the <title> node
- DOM Example is a text node and its parent is the <title> node
- The <h1> and <p> nodes are child nodes of <body> and siblings to each other
- The <head> element is the first child of the <html> element and <body> element is the last child of the <html> element
- The <h1> element is the first child of the <body> element and the <p> element is the last child of the <body> element

JavaScript and DOM

DOM allows JavaScript to manipulate all HTML elements, HTML attributes, and CSS styles. It also allows responding to the events that occur in the page. The DOM allows the following actions with JavaScript:

- Finding HTML elements
- Changing the CSS (Cascading Style Sheets) of HTML elements
- Modifying the content (innerHTML) of HTML elements
- Responding to HTML DOM events
- Adding or removing HTML elements

Finding HTML elements

DOM allows finding HTML elements in the following ways:

- By ID
- By name
- By tag name
- By class name

Finding HTML elements by ID

The getElementById method allows retrieving the elements by IDs, for example:

```
var id = document.getElementById("id1");
```

The method will return the element as an object. If the element is not found, the ID will contain a null value.

Finding HTML elements by tag name

The getElementsByTagName method allows retrieving the elements by tag name, for example:

```
var y = document.getElementsByTagName("p");
```

Finding HTML elements by name

Retrieve the elements by tag name using the `getElementsByTagName` method, as shown in the following example. The `getElementsByName` method allows retrieving the elements by tag name, for example:

```
var y = document.getElementsByName("userName");
```

Finding HTML elements by className

To retrieve the elements by class name using the `getElementsByClassName` method as shown in the following example. The `getElementsByClassName` allows retrieving the elements by class name, for example:

```
var z  = document.getElementsByClassName(names);
```

 Finding elements using the `getElementsByClassName` method does not work in IE 5, 6, 7, and 8.

Changing the HTML content

Changing the content of an HTML element is simple as it can be achieved through changing the `innerHTML` property of an HTML element. Use this syntax:

```
document.getElementById(elementid).innerHTML= new value
```

The following example changes the content of an HTML element:

```html
<html>
  <body>
    <h1 id="headerid">Heading</h1>
    <script>
      varelement=document.getElementById("headerid");
      element.innerHTML="New Heading";
    </script>
  </body>
</html>
```

Changing the HTML attribute

Retrieve the HTML element using the `getElementById` method as shown, in the following example, and change the attribute with a new value of attribute:

```
document.getElementById(elementid).attribute = NewAttributevalue
```

The following example changes the attribute with a new value of attribute:

```
<html>
  <body>
    <img id="logosmall" alt ="Logo">
    <script>
      document.getElementById("logosmall").alt="This is logo";
    </script>
  </body>
</html>
```

Changing the HTML style

To change the style of an HTML element, use the following code:

```
document.getElementById(elementid).style.property= new style
```

The following example changes the style of a `<p>` element:

```
<html>
  <body>
    <p id="pid2">Color!</p>
    <script>
      document.getElementById("pid2").style.color="red";
    </script>
    <p>The paragraph above is changed to red.</p>
  </body>
</html>
```

This example changes the style of the HTML element with `id="pid1"`, when the user clicks on a button:

```
<!DOCTYPE html>
<html>
  <body>
    <h1 id="pid1">My Heading 1</h1>
    <button type="button"
      onclick="document.getElementById('pid1').style.
color='red'">Click
        Me!</button>
  </body>
</html>
```

Responding to an event

DOM allows JavaScript code or function to be executed when an event occurs; for example, when a user hovers over an HTML element:

```
object.onmouseover=function(){SomeJavaScriptCode};
```

Following are a few examples of HTML events:

In the following example, a function is called from the event handler: An event handler allows us to call a JavaScript function, as shown in the following example:

```
<html>
  <head>
    <script>
      function changetext(id) {id.innerHTML="Text is changed!"; }
    </script>
  </head>
  <body>
    <h1 onclick="changetext(this)">Click on this text!</h1>
  </body>
</html>
```

Creating new HTML elements

Create the element node first, and then append it to an existing element:

```
<div id="div1">
  <p id="pid1">This is a paraOne.</p>
  <p id="pid2">This is paraTwo.</p>
</div>
<script>
var para=document.createElement("p");
var node=document.createTextNode("This is new Para.");
para.appendChild(node);
var element=document.getElementById("div1");
element.appendChild(para);
</script>
```

The preceding code can be explained as follows:

- It creates a new `<p>` element
- To add text to the `<p>` element, create a text node first
- Append the text node to the `<p>` element

- It finds an existing element
- It appends a new element to the existing element

Removing an existing HTML element

Before removing the child element, know the parent of the element and then remove it, for example:

```
<div id="dividl">
  <p id="pidl">This is a paragraph.</p>
  <p id="pid2">This is another paragraph.</p>
</div>
<script>
//Find the element with id="dividl":
var parent=document.getElementById("dividl");
//Find the <p> element with id="pidl":
var child=document.getElementById("pidl");
//Remove the child from the parent:
parent.removeChild(child);
</script>
```

The preceding HTML document contains a `<div>` element with two child nodes (two `<p>` elements):

```
<div id="div1">
  Child: 1 <p id="pidl"> This is a paragraph. </p>
  Child: 2 <p id="pid2"> This is another paragraph. </p>
</div>
```

The DOM requires knowing that both the elements and their parent require removing. It does not allow removing the child without its parent's reference. The workaround uses the `parentNode` property of the child object to get the parent and then uses `removeChild` to remove it:

```
var childelement = document.getElementById("pidl");
childelement.parentNode.removeChild(childelement);
```

DOM and QTP

QuickTest Object property for a Web object allows us to get a reference to the DOM object, and can perform any operation on a DOM object. For example, the following code shows that the object on the page allows retrieving the element by name username, that is, the textbox in the next step assigns the value as ashish.

```
Set Obj =
  Browser("Tours").Page("Tours").Object.getElementsByName("userName)
'Get the length of the objects
Print obj.length
'
obj(0).value="ashish"
```

The following code snippet shows various operations that can be performed using the Object property of the web object:

```
'Retrieve all the link elements in a web page
Set links = Browser ("Mercury Tours").Page("Mercury
  Tours").Object.links
 'Length property provide total number of links
For i =0 to links.length -1
  Print links(i).toString() 'Print the value of the links
Next
Get the web edit object and set the focus on it
Set MyWebEdit = Browser("Tours").Page("Tours").WebEdit("username").
Object
MyWebEdit.focus
'Retrieve the html element by its name
 obj = Browser("Tours").Page("Tours").Object.
getElementsByName("userName"
  )
 'set the value to the retrieved object
 obj.value ="ashish"
'Retrieve the total number of the images in the web pages
set  images =  Browser("Mercury Tours").Page("Mercury
  Tours").Object.images
print  images.length
'Clicking on the Image
obj = Browser("Tours").Page("Mercury
  Tours").Object.getElementsByName("login")
obj.click
'Selecting the value from the drop down using selectedIndex method
 Browser("Flight").Page("Flight).WebList("pass.0.meal").Object.
selectedIndex =1
```

```
'Click on the check box
Browser("Flight").Page("Flight").WebCheckBox("ticketLess").Object.
  click
```

Firing an event

QTP allows firing of the events on the web objects:

```
Browser("The Fishing Website fishing").Page("The Fishing Website
  fishing").Link("Link").FireEvent "onmouseover"
```

The following example uses the FireEvent method to trigger the onpropertychange event on a form:

```
Browser("New Page").Page("New Page").WebElement("html
  tag:=Form").FireEvent "onpropertychange"
```

QTP allows executing JavaScript code. There are two JavaScript functions that allow us to interact with web pages. We can retrieve objects and perform the actions on them or we can retrieve the properties from the element on the pages:

RunScript executes the JavaScript code, passed as an argument to this function.

The following example shows how the RunScript method calls the ImgCount method, which returns the number of images in the page:

```
length = Browser("Mercury Tours").Page("Mercury
  Tours").RunScript("ImgCount(); function ImageCount() {var list
    = document.getElementsByTagName('img'); return
      list.length;}")
print "The total number of images on the page is " & length
```

RunScriptsFormFile uses the full path of the JavaScript files to execute it. The location can be an absolute or relative filesystem path or a quality center path.

The following is a sample JavaScript file (logo.js):

```
var myNode = document.getElementById("lga");
myNode.innerHTML = '';
```

Use the logo.js file, as shown in the following code:

```
Browser("Browser").Page("page").RunScriptFromFile "c:\logo.js"
'Check that the Web page behaves correctly
If Browser("Browser").Page("page").Image("Image").Exist Then
    Reporter.ReportEvent micFail, "Failed to remove logo"
End If
```

The preceding example uses the `RunScriptFromFile` method to remove a DOM element from a web page and checks if the page still behaves correctly when the DOM element has been removed.

Using XPath

XPath allows navigating and finding elements and attributes in an HTML document. XPath uses path expressions to navigate in HTML documents. QTP allows XPath to create the object description, for example:

```
xpath:=//input[@type='image' and contains(@name,'findFlights')
```

In the following section, we will learn the various XPath terminologies and methodologies to find the objects using XPath.

XPath terminology

XPath uses various terms to define elements and their relationships among HTML elements, as shown in the following table:

Atomic values	Atomic values are nodes with no children or parent
Ancestors	A node's parent, parent's parent, and so on
Descendants	A node's children, children's children, and so on
Parent	Each element and attribute has one parent
Children	Element nodes may have zero, one, or more children
Siblings	Nodes that have the same parent

Selecting nodes

A path expression allows selecting nodes in a document. The commonly used path expressions are shown in the following table:

Symbol	Meaning
/(slash)	Select elements relative to the root node
//(double slash)	Select nodes in the document from the current node that match the selection irrespective of its position
.(dot)	Represents the current node
..	Represents the parent of the current node
@	Represents an attribute
nodename	Selects all nodes with the name "nodename"

Slash (/) is used in the beginning and it defines an absolute path; for example, /html/head/title returns the title tag. It defines ancestor and descendant relationships if used in the middle; for example, //div/table returns the div containing a table.

Double slash (//) is used to find a node in any location; for example, //table returns all the tables. It defines a descendant relationship if used in the middle; for example, /html//title returns the title tag, which is descendant of the html tag.

Refer to the following table to see a few more examples with their meanings:

Expression	Meaning
//a	Find all anchor tags
//a//img	List the images that are inside a link
//img/@alt	Show all the alt tags
//a/@href	Show the href attribute for every link
//a[@*]	Anchor tab with any attribute
//title/text() or /html/head/title/text()	Get the title of a page
//img[@alt]	List the images that have alt tags
//img[not(@alt)]	List the images that don't have alt tags
//*[@id='mainContent']	Get an element with a particular CSS ID
//div [not(@id="div1")]	Make an array element from the XPath
//p/..	Selects the parent element of p (paragraph) child
XXX[@att]	Selects all the child elements of XXX with an attribute named att
./@* for example, //script/./@*	Finds all attribute values of current element

Predicates

A predicate is embedded in square brackets and is used to find out specific node(s) or a node that contains a specific value:

- //p[@align]: This allows finding all the tags that have align attribute value as center
- //img[@alt]: This allows finding all the img (image) tags that contain the alt tag

- `//table[@border]`: This allows finding all the `table` tags that contain `border` attributes
- `//table[@border >1]`: This finds the table with border value greater than 1

Retrieve the table row using the complete path:

`//body/div/table/tbody/tr[1]`

Get the name of the parent of `//body/div/table/..` (parent of the `table` tag)

`//body/div/table/..[name()]`

Path expression	Result
`//div/p[1]`	Selects the first paragraph element that is the child of the `div` element
`//div/p [last()]`	Selects the last paragraph element that is the child of the `div` element
`//div/p[last()-1]`	Selects the second last paragraph element that is the child of the `div` element
`//div/p[position()<3]`	Selects the first two paragraph elements that are children of the `div` element
`//script[@language]`	Selects all script element(s) with an attribute named as `language`
`//script[@ language='javascript']`	Selects all the script elements that have an attribute named `language` with a value of JavaScript
`//div/p[text()>45.00]`	Selects all the paragraph elements of the `div` element that have a text element with a value greater than 45.00

Selecting unknown nodes

Apart from selecting the specific nodes in XPath, XPath allows us to select the group of HTML elements using `*`, `@`, and `node()` functions.

- `*` represents an element node
- `@` represents the attribute
- `node()` represents any node

The previous mentioned elements allow selecting the unknown nodes; for example:

- `/div/*` selects all the child nodes of a `div` element
- `//*` selects all the elements in a document
- `//script[@*]` selects all the title elements which contain attributes

Selecting several paths

Use **union | operator** in XPath expressions for allowing to select several paths, as shown in the following table:

Path expression	Action
`//div|/p	//div/span`	Selects all the paragraph and `span` elements of the `div` element
`//p	//span`	Selects all the p (paragraph) and `span` elements in the document

Axes in XPath

An axis allows defining a node which is relative to its current node. The following is the list of the axes in XPath:

- self
- parent
- attribute
- child
- Ancestor and ancestor-or-self
- Descendant and descendant-or-self
- Following and following-sibling
- Preceding and preceding-sibling
- namespace

Locating a element using location path

A location of the element is represented in two ways using absolute and relative paths.

Each step is evaluated against the nodes in the current node. The syntax looks like the following syntax:

```
axisname::nodetest[predicate]
```

An axis defines the tree-relationship between selected nodes and current node.

A node-test allows us to identify node(s) within an axis.

Zero or more predicates allow further refining of the selected node set.

Take a look at the following example:

```
//input[ancestor-or-self::*[@name='userName']]
```

In the preceding example, `ancestor-or-self is an axes, ::*` is the nodetest and `[@name='userName']` is the predicate, allowing us to search all `ancestor-or-self` elements whose attribute names are `userName` contained in the `input` type element `//input[ansector-or-self::*[@name='userName']]`.

Axes allow finding the descendant of the element; for example:

`//div[descendant::p]` allows us to find all the `div` elements having descendant as paragraph.

`descendant::p` axes allow finding the ancestor and descendant of the element, for example, finding all the ancestors of button or finding all the `div` whose descendants are `table`.

```
//input[Ancestor::div[@align='center']]
//div[descendant::table]
```

Use of the XPath functions:

- `//div/text()`: This retrieves the text from the `div` tags using `text` functions
- `//div/node()`: Getting all the nodes under `div` tags using the `node` function

To get the descendant, XPath function `start-with` finds the value that starts with `//a[starts-with(@href,'http://ads')`.

Find all tags that contains the `style` attribute `//*[@style]`.

Operators in XPath

The XPath expressions use operators to build the conditions to be evaluated. The following is the list of XPath operators:

Operator category	Operator	Description
Mathematical	+	Addition
	-	Subtraction
	*	Multiplication
	Div	Div Division
	MOD	MOD Modulus (division remainder)
Equality and comparison	=	Equal
	!=	Not equal
	<	Less than
	<=	Less than or equal to
	>	Greater than
	>=	Greater than or equal to
Logical	Or	Logical Or
	And	Logical And
Two node sets	| Union	Computes two node sets

The following table shows some examples for using the operators in XPath expressions:

Expression	Action
`//input	//div/input/..`	Input union input where `div` is its parent
`//table[@border>=1]`	Retrieves the tables that have border greater than 1
`//table[@id=3]/td[2]/text()+1`	Retrieves the text from the third row and second column and adds 1 to it
`//tr[@id=1] and //tr[@id=3]`	Returns true if both expression are true

Example of using XPath in finding the siblings which allow finding the object related to their siblings and not to their location:

```
<html>
<Body>
<br><br>
<table name="maintable" border="1">
<th>Item</th><th>Quantity</th><th>Price</th><th></th>
<tr id=1 width="600px">
<td> HP LoadRuuner </td>
<td > 01 </td>
<td> $27 </td>
<td> <input type="button" value="AddToCart"> </td>
</tr>
<tr id=2 width="600px">
<td> HP Quality Center </td>
<td> 01 </td>
<td> $29 </td>
<td> <input type="button" value="AddToCart"> </td>
</tr>
<tr id=3 width="600px">
<td > HP QuickTest Professional </td>
<td > 01 </td>
<td> $25 </td>
<td> <input type="button" value="AddToCart"> </td>
</tr>
</table>
</body>
</html>
```

Add the code to the file and save it as an `.html` file. Click on the **AddToCart** button.

Remove the following recorded script:

```
Browser("Browser").Page("Page").WebButton("AddToCart").Click
```

Replace and use the following script:

```
Browser("Browser").Page("Page").WebButton("xpath:=//td[contains(te
    xt(),'HP QuickTest')]/following-sibling::td[3]/input").Click
```

This preceding script allows clicking on the button (**AddToCart**), which is the sibling of the HP QuickTest Professional text. To click on the **AddToCart** button, which is the sibling of HP Quality Center text, use the following code:

```
Browser("Browser").Page("Page").WebButton("xpath:=//td[contains(te
  xt(),'HP Quality Center')]/following-
    sibling::td[3]/input").Click
```

XPath can be implemented in the QTP Scripts. The following section explains the various usages of XPath in a web page. Examples of the usage of XPath are:

- Entering a value in the text box
- Selecting the value from a drop-down list
- Clicking on images and buttons
- Finding objects by ID, tag name, name, and attributes
- Allowing to extract the information for validation
- Dealing with duplicate objects as array subscripts

Key steps to create a framework using XPath are:

1. Identify the flow to be recorded.
2. Create OR (create OR for each page or use the object description).
3. Identify the XPath that identifies the object uniquely.
4. Define the XPath that allows us to retrieve an element and defines it as a constant.
5. Use them as object descriptions.

Tips for scripting using XPath:

- Use descriptive programming (use `index` property) for handling duplicate objects or array subscripts in XPath expressions
- XPath allows the use of index for collection of elements
- Retrieve `innerHTML` with `GetROProperty` to get the values
- Define object description using XPath as constant, allowing easier maintenance, and only a single place to change and no need to change all over the script

Summary

In this chapter, we have learned about various concepts and examples. The knowledge of DOM, JavaScript, and XPath is very handy for creating scripts. The XPath and DOM are the least used concepts in the QTP for script creation and validation, but these are helpful in creating manual checkpoints by retrieving the data from the web pages conveniently. Path is a really good way to navigate your site when there are no IDs on elements that you need to work with or near the element you want to work with. The next chapter talks about capturing and sharing the lessons learned during the test automation framework designing, and implementing them for future reference.

7
Capturing the Lessons Learned

In the previous chapters we have learned the various techniques used by QTP for creating scripts and framework components and designing and maintaining frameworks. In this chapter, we will focus on capturing the lessons learned and their utilization for future use, which will be covered in the following topics:

- Preparing for the lessons to be learned
- Collecting and documenting the learning
- Best practices for collecting the lessons learned
- Discussing the lessons learned
- Storing and sharing the lessons learned document

Preparing for the lessons to be learned

An organization that allows capturing of the lessons learned as a process becomes more efficient and effective in executing test automation projects from conception to completion. Ensure that the knowledge gained during the test automation life cycle should be captured in a way that it becomes effective for future references.

We will be organizing the lessons learned for the following areas:

- People
- Process
- Framework design

Test managers and automation leads have responsibilities towards test automation, the automation team, as well as organizing and refining the processes. At each meeting, they should ask a series of questions regarding the following topics:

- What has been achieved against the defined goals for test automation
- What are the best ways to utilize the lessons learned for next releases and future projects

The discussion should be organized around the following three areas:

- **People**: What are the skills, knowledge, and experience we have gained about staffing and automation design; these will help in future releases and projects
- **Process**: The tools, techniques, or practices that were used for the automation and the ones should be used or avoided for future projects
- **Design**: How design and reusable libraries have helped in achieving goals and how to make them more useful for future releases and projects

Collecting and documenting learning

We have to collect and store information by its category; the key discussion areas for which we will capture the information are stated in the following sections:

Key challenges

Every project has some challenges. Documenting these challenges and the methods of their mitigation will be of great help in future. These challenges can be related to people, tool technology, skills, or processes.

What went well

When positive outcomes are captured and documented, they become guidelines for future projects.

What can be better

When we capture what can be better, it suggests how proactively we can use these lessons to overcome the challenges already faced — these will help in risk identification and mitigation. Some of them can even be chosen as the goals for future projects.

Chapter 7

Best practices for collecting lessons learned

Automation team members always possess the key to learning at the back of their minds; it is always in the best interests of the individual, project, and the organization. It is important to bring these lessons into writing by documenting them.

Start capturing early

We should start the capture learning early, right from the conception phase. This allows us to capture most of the learning without losing the information due to procrastination.

Documentation and ensuring reusability

It is important to document the lesson(s) even if not organized initially. Only capturing and documenting the lessons learned is not enough. You need to ensure that these lessons are saved and available for reuse; they should be easily accessible across various teams.

Discussing lessons learned

The lessons learned revolve around the following topics:

- **Agenda**: Set up a meeting with the key stakeholders to discuss the lessons learned for the test automation. Begin with setting up the meeting agenda.
- **Project details**: Here you will introduce the project and its details, such as the technologies and tools used, domain of application, and team size and composition. The details for the key stakeholders can be summed up as follows:
    - **Customer**: This field will hold the customer's name.
    - **Engagement/Project Name**: The corresponding project name is to be mentioned.
    - **Test Manager**: This field will hold the test manager's name.
    - **Project Manager**: The project manager's name is to be entered.

- **Challenges**: Brief the team on the key challenges faced and how you mitigated them. Encourage every team member to participate and assertively speak about their observation and learning. Challenges can belong to any of these areas, including technical, process, people, and skill issues.

- **What went well**: You need to brief everyone on what went well. This will be useful for future references as best practices or reusable assets. These assets could be in the form of documentation or code libraries. The lessons learned will become the key reference points for later projects.

- **What can be better**: Mention the areas in which the team could have performed better; these lessons are very important for estimating the effort, risk mitigation, skill development and training, and improving all aspects of test automation for future projects.

Storing and sharing lessons learned

Mature organizations allow the storing of project documents and reusable assets and provide access to them for future projects. It is important to provide appropriate access to the documents with other teams across the organization. Some organizations have a **Software Process Engineering Group (SPEG)**. Some team members of the SPEG group review the documents and libraries before the artifacts are submitted to the central repository.

Summary

Spreading knowledge and learning allows the growth of maturity for test automation individuals as well as for the organization. This chapter tells us about the practices and tips around the lessons learned and their importance, all of which are applicable for any test automation tool or practices, including QTP.

Index

BPT 59, 97
Business Process Testing. *See* BPT

C

capacity attribute 12
CaptureBitmap method 104
case sensitivity, VBScript syntax rules 42
checklist
  reviewing, for pre-deployment 103-105
checkpoints
  about 31, 44, 45
  accessibility checkpoint 33
  Bitmap checkpoint 32
  database checkpoint 32
  image checkpoint 31
  page checkpoint 32
  regular expression 56, 57
  standard checkpoint 31
  table checkpoint 32
  Text Area checkpoint 32
  text checkpoint 32
  XML checkpoint 33
CheckProperty
  regular expression 57-60
code blocks
  key features 41
comments, VBScript syntax rules 43
compatibility attribute 13
custom logs
  about 105
  logging, enabling 105, 106
  logs, disabling 106
  logs, filtering 106
  test version, versus debug version 108

D

database checkpoint 32
data-driven framework
  about 73
  creating, datatable object used 74
  creating, steps 74
  data, accessing in QTP 74
  data, fetching 75
  FileSystemObject object model 78-80
  iteration 74
  parameter 74

test, parameterizing 76
variable 74
Data-driven framework 70
datatypes, VBScript
  Boolean 64
  Byte 64
  Currency 64
  Date (Time) 64
  Double 64
  Empty 64
  Error 64
  Integer 64
  Long 64
  Null 64
  Object 64
  Sin4gle 64
  String 64
Debug from Step option 102
debugging
  about 101
  custom logs 105-108
  planning 101
  QTP using 102-105
debugging, QTP used
  Debug from action option 102
  Debug from Step option 102
  functional library, debugging 103
  pre deployment checklist, reviewing 103-
    105
  Run from action option 102
  Run from step option 102
  Run to action option 103
  Run to Step option 102
Debug variable 105, 106
decomposition 88
Default object types option 27
deployment 109
deployment phase
  key steps 11
descriptive programming
  about 51
  dynamic programming 51
  regular expression 56
  static programming 51
design
  goals 15

design, modular framework
about 84
application, analyzing 87
cohesion, increasing 86, 87
concise scripts 85
coupling, decreasing 86, 87
design, creating 87
environment, setting up 88
extensibility 84
high cohesion 85
loose coupling, achieving 85
maintainability 84
Object Repository, creating 89
readability 84
reusability 85
script-level functions, creating 89
testing 89
test-level components, creating 89
Document Object Model. *See* **DOM**
Do Loop 68, 69
DOM
about 113
and JavaScript 115
and QTP 120
HTML DOM 113
DOM actions, with JavaScript
event, responding to 118
existing HTML element, removing 119
HTML attribute, modifying 116
HTML content, modifying 116
HTML elements, finding 115
HTML elements, finding by ID 115
HTML elements, finding by name 116
HTML elements, finding by tag name 115
HTML style, modifying 117
new HTML elements, creating 118
duplicate objects 54
dynamic programming 53-55
dynamic synchronization 49-51

E

enhancement
about 111
key steps 111
Environment libraries 94
Environment.xml file 39

equality and comparison operators, XPath
127
Err object
properties 58
Error libraries 94
Expert View option 102

F

feasibility study
about 8
applying 8
FileSystemObject object model
about 78
data, writing to 78-80
file, manipulating 78
Filter property 105, 106
For each Next loop 69
framework
about 70
Automation goals 70
Data-driven type 70
hybrid 70
keyword-driven 70
linear type 70
modular framework 70
recording process 71, 72
test automation framework 70
framework design
goals 15
functional library
debugging 103
function procedure 44

G

getElementsByClassName method 116
GetROProperty method 20
GetTOProperty method 20

H

HTML
attributes, changing 116
content, changing 116
elements, creating 118
styles, changing 117

Q

QTP
about 19
and DOM 120
event, finding 121
framework creating, points 63
object model 20
QTP linear framework approach
about 71
creating 71, 72
Quality Centre (QC) 59
QuickTest. *See* **QTP**
QuickTest object model 20
QuickTest Professional. *See* **QTP**

R

recombination 88
record
process 21
recovery scenario
about 60
post-recovery option 60
recovery operations 60
trigger event 60
regular expression
about 55
in checkpoint 56, 57
in CheckProperty 57-59
in descriptive programming 56
release phase
key steps 11
reliability attribute 12
replay
process 21, 22
reporter object
about 35
Reporter.RunStatus object 36
Reporter object 105-108
Reporter.RunStatus object 36
ReportEvent method 35, 107
ReportNote method 35
reusable actions
external actions 37
non reusable actions 37
purpose 37

reusable actions 37
rfDisableAll option 106
rfEnableAll option 105
Run from Action option 102
Run from Step option 102
Run Result window 105-108
RunScript method 121
Run to Action option 103
Run to step option 102

S

script design
goals 15
script development
application, analyzing 22
scripts, enhancing 31
steps 22
test objects, adding to OR 22, 23
test step, adding 28
script/library
maintaining 110
scripts
checkpoints 31, 32
designing 10
developing 10
enhancing 31
environment variables, using 38
error handling 37
parameterization 38
reporter object 35
reusable actions 36
synchronization 33
Selected object only option 27
Selected object types option 27
Software Process Engineering Group
(SPEG) 134
spaces, VBScript syntax rules 43
standard checkpoint 31
static programming 52
structure advantages, modular framework
better performance 84
control over resources 84
easier communication 84
facilitates specialization 84

Thank you for buying
Designing and Implementing Test Automation
Frameworks with QTP

About Packt Publishing

Packt, pronounced 'packed', published its first book "Mastering phpMyAdmin for Effective MySQL Management" in April 2004 and subsequently continued to specialize in publishing highly focused books on specific technologies and solutions.

Our books and publications share the experiences of your fellow IT professionals in adapting and customizing today's systems, applications, and frameworks. Our solution based books give you the knowledge and power to customize the software and technologies you're using to get the job done. Packt books are more specific and less general than the IT books you have seen in the past. Our unique business model allows us to bring you more focused information, giving you more of what you need to know, and less of what you don't.

Packt is a modern, yet unique publishing company, which focuses on producing quality, cutting-edge books for communities of developers, administrators, and newbies alike. For more information, please visit our website: www.packtpub.com.

About Packt Enterprise

In 2010, Packt launched two new brands, Packt Enterprise and Packt Open Source, in order to continue its focus on specialization. This book is part of the Packt Enterprise brand, home to books published on enterprise software – software created by major vendors, including (but not limited to) IBM, Microsoft and Oracle, often for use in other corporations. Its titles will offer information relevant to a range of users of this software, including administrators, developers, architects, and end users.

Writing for Packt

We welcome all inquiries from people who are interested in authoring. Book proposals should be sent to author@packtpub.com. If your book idea is still at an early stage and you would like to discuss it first before writing a formal book proposal, contact us; one of our commissioning editors will get in touch with you.

We're not just looking for published authors; if you have strong technical skills but no writing experience, our experienced editors can help you develop a writing career, or simply get some additional reward for your expertise.

[PACKT] enterprise
PUBLISHING
professional expertise distilled

Instant Sikuli Test Automation

ISBN: 978-1-78216-787-7   Paperback: 54 pages

Discover automated application testing techniques for anything that is visible on the computer screen

1. Learn something new in an Instant! A short, fast, focused guide delivering immediate results

2. Write simple tests using the Sikuli IDE

3. Construct a framework for running your tests and reporting results

4. Learn best practices for building reusable Sikuli scripts and sharing capabilities between them

Selenium Testing Tools Cookbook

ISBN: 978-1-84951-574-0   Paperback: 326 pages

Over 90 recipes to build, maintain, and improve test automation with Selenium WebDriver

1. Learn to leverage the power of Selenium WebDriver with simple examples that illustrate real world problems and their workarounds

2. Each sample demonstrates key concepts allowing you to advance your knowledge of Selenium WebDriver in a practical and incremental way

3. Explains testing of mobile web applications with Selenium Drivers for platforms such as iOS and Android

Please check **www.PacktPub.com** for information on our titles

Learning Software Testing with Test Studio

ISBN: 978-1-84968-890-1   Paperback: 376 pages

Embark on the exciting journey of test automation, execution, and reporting in Test Studio with this practical tutorial

1. Learn to use Test Studio to design and automate tests valued with their functionality and maintainability

2. Run manual and automated test suites and view reports on them

3. Filled with practical examples, snapshots and Test Studio hints to automate and substitute throwaway tests with long term frameworks

Python Testing: Beginner's Guide

ISBN: 978-1-84719-884-6   Paperback: 256 pages

An easy and convenient approach to testing your powerful Python projects

1. Covers everything you need to test your code in Python

2. Easiest and enjoyable approach to learn Python testing

3. Write, execute, and understand the result of tests in the unit test framework

4. Packed with step-by-step examples and clear explanations

Please check **www.PacktPub.com** for information on our titles

Lightning Source UK Ltd.
Milton Keynes UK
UKOW02f2301170114

224780UK00003BA/108/P